Henri Kling

Schule für Waldhorn

Europäischer Musikverlag

Henri Kling

Schule für Waldhorn

ISBN/EAN: 9783956980947

Auflage: 1

Erscheinungsjahr: 2015

Erscheinungsort: Norderstedt, Deutschland

Hergestellt in Europa, USA, Kanada, Australien, Japan
Europäischer Musikverlag in Hansebooks GmbH, Norderstedt

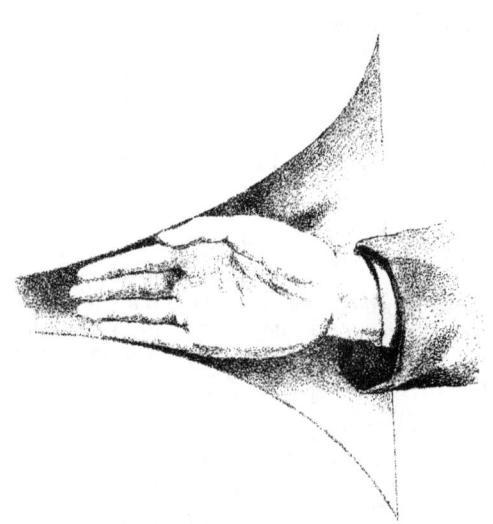

VORREDE

Bei der Abfassung dieser Hornschule glaubte ich über die Grundelemente der Musik hinweggehen zu können, denn wer sich diesem Instrument widmen will, muß über dies Rüstzeug von vornherein verfügen. Es ist wirklich ganz unmöglich, das Hornblasen ohne musikalische Vorkenntnisse erlernen zu wollen.

Ich halte es auch für überflüssig, hier den Schüler über die Haltung des Hornes oder über die Beschaffenheit des Mundstückes belehren zu wollen. Dies ist Aufgabe des Lehrers; denn er ist allein in der Lage, den Schüler über die Haltung des Instrumentes und über die Führung der Hand in der Stürze wirklich zu unterrichten. Die richtige Haltung der Hand in der Stürze ist sehr wesentlich, weil sie von Einfluß bei der Bildung des Tones ist.

Diese Schule ist für Wald- (Naturhorn) und Ventilhorn geschrieben. Ich empfehle dringend, zuerst das Waldhorn zu erlernen, um wirklich in den Besitz eines schönen Tones zu gelangen. Leider haben ihn nur sehr wenige Hornisten, weil sie das Instrument nach Art des Pistons oder der Posaune behandeln und es dadurch seines ihm eigenen Charakters berauben.

Ein Teil der in diese Schule aufgenommenen Stücke ist für zwei Hörner geschrieben. Spielen die Schüler abwechselnd beide Partien mit dem gleichen Ansatz, so lernen sie das Instrument in seinem vollen Umfang wirklich kennen. Der Schüler übe nur die Stücke, die sein augenblickliches Können nicht übersteigen. Er gehe auch nur stufenweise, von Lektion zur Lektion, vor und halte streng die Reihenfolge der einzelnen Übungen inne. Der Schüler sollte mit Üben aufhören, wenn er merkt, daß er ermüdet und daß die Schönheit des Tones nachläßt. Machen wir uns den Grundsatz des berühmten Hornisten Dauprat zu eigen, der einmal sagt: »Arbeitet wenig auf einmal, aber oft«.

Und so hoffe ich, daß die Mühe, die ich an dieses Werk setzte, nicht vergeblich war, und daß die Schule zu ihrem Teile mit dazu beiträgt, wirklich gute Hornisten heranzubilden.

Allgemeine Bemerkungen

1. Die Wahl des Mundstückes ist von größter Wichtigkeit. Sie muß sich nach der Stärke oder der Schwäche

PREFACE

In the compilation of the present Method for the Horn, I have not considered it requisite to deal with the elementary principles of music, seeing that those intending to devote themselves to the study of the instrument would necessarily have had to master them beforehand. It would, indeed, be absolutely useless to attempt playing the horn without such preliminary musical knowledge.

For a similar reason, I have likewise dispensed with lengthy observations and explanations concerning the correct way of holding the horn, the proportions of the mouthpiece and other particulars, which I consider superfluous here. They are all of them matters of detail properly appertaining to the province of the teacher, who must show the pupil how to hold his instrument and the proper way of inserting his hand in the bell.

The latter manipulation is a most essential point in horn playing, as the quality of the tone is thereby influenced and modified.

The present Method is intended both for the Natural or Stop-Horn and for the Valve or Ventil-Horn.

In order to obtain a thorough mastery in horn playing, it is extremely advisable to begin with the study of the Natural Horn, for the purpose of acquiring the true quality of tone characteristic of the instrument and which is attained by but few hornists. They generally treat the instrument as though it were a Cornet à pistons or a trombone, thereby depriving it of its genuine character.

Some of the pieces contained in this work are written for two horns, to enable pupils to play both parts alternately and thus become acquainted with the entire compass of the instrument; the reasonable compass, that is, as it has been established by the most eminent professors.

The pupil should only attempt those pieces which are proportionate to his powers and study the exercises contained in the present "School" consecutively, in the order in which they are presented.

"Short practices often repeated" — the maxim of the celebrated hornist Dauprat — shall also be our own motto.

"As soon as the lips are getting fatigued and the tone becomes uncertain", practice should be discontinued.

I venture to hope, that the care I have bestowed upon this work will not have been expended unprofitably, and that, supplemented by the efforts of teachers, it may be the means of

PRÉFACE

En composant cette Méthode de Cor, je ne me suis pas cru obligé de donner les principes de la musique, car les Personnes qui se destinent à l'étude de cet instrument, doivent nécessairement les posséder d'avance, et vouloir jouer du Cor, sans avoir solfié, serait vouloir une chose absolument impossible.

Je me suis aussi dispensé d'écrire de longues observations, pour les élèves, soit sur la «tenue du Cor» soit sur les «proportions de l'embouchure» et autres recommandations que je trouve superflues, car tout ceci doit être l'affaire du professeur, c'est lui qui doit choisir l'instrument et l'embouchure, et enseigner à l'élève comment on doit tenir le Cor, et faire agir la main dans le pavillon.

Bien tenir la main dans le pavillon, est une chose essentielle, car elle influe sur la qualité du son.

Cette méthode est composée pour Cor simple (cor d'harmonie), c'est-à-dire, sans pistons ni cylindres, et pour Cor chromatique, c'est-à-dire, avec pistons ou cylindres.

Pour bien savoir jouer du Cor, il serait urgent d'apprendre d'abord le Cor simple, afin de s'approprier la qualité du son sur cet instrument, que bien peu de cornistes possèdent, parce qu'ils jouent du cor à la façon du Cornet à pistons ou du Trombone, et lui ôtent ainsi son caractère propre.

Une partie des morceaux contenus dans cette méthode sont écrits pour deux cors, afin que les élèves jouant alternativement les deux parties, avec la même embouchure, parviennent à connaître toute l'étendue de l'instrument, je dis, l'étendue raisonnable, telle que nos meilleurs artistes l'ont maintenant determinée.

L'élève ne doit exécuter que de la musique proportionnée à sa force, et par conséquent s'astreindre à n'étudier les leçons de cette méthode que successivement et dans l'ordre ou elle sont présentées.

«Travailler peu et souvent», voilà la devise du célèbre corniste Dauprat, qu'elle soit donc aussi la nôtre.

«Aussitôt que les lèvres se fatiguent et que le son s'altère» on doit s'arrêter.

J'ose espérer que les soins donnés à cet ouvrage ne seront pas jugés inutiles, et que joints à ceux de Messieurs les Professeurs, ils pourront contribuer à former de bons élèves pour un instrument, qui est sans contredit un des plus importants dans l'orchestre moderne.

der Lippen des Schülers richten. Es ist aber unmöglich, hierfür irgendwelche Richtlinien zu geben. Der Schüler muß sich hierbei der Erfahrung seines Lehrers, den er sich am besten vor Beginn des Studiums wählt, anvertrauen.

2. Das Mundstück wird an die Lippen auf leichte natürliche Weise in der Mitte des Mundes angesetzt und ja nicht etwa nach den Mundwinkeln zu. Bei der Bildung des Tones muß das Mundstück ziemlich fest an die Lippen gedrückt werden.

3. Will man den Ton frei angeben, dann muß man eine genügend große Öffnung zum Durchblasen der Luft zwischen der Unter- und Oberlippe lassen, auch deshalb, weil die Zunge hinreichenden Spielraum braucht, um die Töne auf natürliche Art einmal stark, einmal schwach anschlagen zu können. Man hüte sich davor, die Backen aufzublasen, oder das Gesicht zu verzerren. Bei absteigenden Noten gebe man mit den Lippen ein wenig nach, bei aufsteigenden ziehe man die Lippen umso fester an, doch ohne sonst den Ansatz irgendwie zu verändern.

4. Die Haltung der Hand in der Stürze des Instrumentes ist nicht minder wichtig. Erstens beeinflußt sie die Schönheit des Tones, dann erleichtert sie aber auch die Ausführung schwieriger Passagen. Dies gilt sowohl für das Natur-, wie für das Ventilhorn. (Siehe Abbildung Nr. 3.)

5. Die Wahl eines guten Instrumentes ist dem Urteil eines geschickten Lehrers zu überlassen, der das Horn vor dem Ankauf genau probieren und untersuchen muß, ob es allen Anforderungen an Reinheit und schönem Ton entspricht. Besonders bei Ventilhörnern achte man auf reine Stimmung.

6. Beim Atemholen muß man sich daran gewöhnen, nur Luft zu schöpfen, wenn eine Pause vorhanden ist oder aber nur dann, wenn wirklich der Atem nicht ausreicht. Hierbei darf man das Instrument aber nicht absetzen.

Zum Schluß empfehle ich noch das Ausgießen des Speichels, welcher sich in den Röhren leicht ansammelt, nie außer acht zu lassen. Dadurch wird nämlich das Überschlagen der Töne verhindert, was so oft bei mindergeschulten Hornisten vorkommt.

forming good pupils and increasing the number of competent performers on an instrument which may be justly described as one of the most important in our modern orchestras.

General Observations

1. The selection of the mouthpiece is a matter of the greatest moment and must be determined by the relative thickness or thinness of the pupils lips. It is impossible to give precise theoretical or practical indications on this subject; it should be left entirely in the hands of the experienced teacher, who will have been chosen before study is commenced.

2. The contact of the mouthpiece with the lips should be an easy and natural one, in the centre of the mouth — not by any means tending towards the corners of the mouth — pressing the mouthpiece rather firmly to the lips in producing the tone.

3. In order to produce the tone freely, the lips should be left sufficiently wide apart to allow for a passage of the air and also that the tip of the tongue may have free play to produce the tones in a natural manner, both loudly and softly, without inflating of the cheeks or other contortions of the face.

4. The proper position of the hand in the bell of the instrument is likewise a matter of the utmost importance, both as affecting the quality of the tone and facilitating the execution of brilliant and difficult passages, whether it be on the Natural or on the Ventil-horn. (See diagram No. 3.)

5. The choice of a good instrument, which — and this applies particularly to the chromatic horn — must be accurately toned, should be entrusted to judgment of a competent teacher, who will be careful to test the instrument in regard to the essential conditions of purity and good quality of its tone, before a final selection is made.

6. Concerning respiration, the pupil will have to accustom himself to taking breath, during the progress of a performance, in such places only where it becomes a physical necessity. In no case, however, should the mouthpiece be removed from the lips, unless it be warranted — as for instance in a symphonic work — by the occurrence of many bars of rests.

Finally, I would recommend careful attention being paid to the ejection of the moisture which easily accumulates in the tubes during performance, so as to avoid the unpleasant couacs with which mediocre hornists have rendered us familiar, whose musical training generally and study of the art of horn-playing in particular have been altogether problematical.

Observations générales

1. Le choix d'une embouchure est de la plus haute importance, ce choix se fait suivant la grosseur et la finesse des lèvres de l'élève, il est impossible de donner à ce sujet des indications précises, soit théoriques, soit pratiques, il faut pour cela se rapporter entièrement à l'expérience du professeur que l'on aura préalablement choisi, avant que d'entreprendre l'étude du cor.

2. La tenue de l'embouchure sur les lèvres doit se faire d'une manière aisée, au milieu de la bouche et non vers les coins, en y appliquant assez fortement l'embouchure afin de pouvoir émettre un son.

3. Pour émettre un son, d'une manière franche, il faut laisser une ouverture suffisante entre la lèvre inférieure et la lèvre supérieure pour le passage de l'air, en sorte que le bout de la langue puisse aisément circuler, afin de produire des sons, d'une façon naturelle, tantôt avec force, tantôt avec douceur, sans gonfler les joues, ni faire des grimaces quel conques. Si l'on veut descendre, on lâchera les lèvres, et on les serrera si l'on veut monter, mais sans rien changer à la tenue de l'embouchure.

4. La tenue de la main dans le pavillon de l'instrument est aussi d'une importance capitale, pour la qualité du son d'abord, puis pour l'agilité et la facilité dans l'exécution de passages brillants et difficiles, soit sur le cor simple soit sur le cor à pistons ou à cylindres.
(Voyez figure Nr. 3.)

5. Le choix d'un bon instrument qui soit accordé d'une manière juste, surtout en ce qui concerne le cor chromatique, est à soumettre à la compétence d'un habile professeur qui doit l'essayer avant l'achat, afin de s'assurer s'il est d'une bonne facture, et s'il peut remplir les conditions indispensables soit sous le rapport de la justesse soit sous celui de la qualité du son.

6. En ce qui concerne la respiration, il faut s'appliquer a respirer dans le courent d'un morceau qu'aux endroits ou la nécessité se fera absolument sentir, mais sans ôter l'embouchure des lèvres, à moins que, comme dans une symphonie, il y ait beaucoup de mesures tacet.

Et pour dernière recommandation je dirai qu'il faut toujours avoir soin d'ôter l'eau qui s'amasse facilement pendant l'exécution, afin d'éviter les couacs si fréquents chez la plupart des cornistes médiocres, dont l'éducation musicale et les études sur l'art de jouer du cor ont été à peu près nulles.

INHALT	Seite
3 Abbildungen: Die Haltung des Horns	
Vorrede	
Vorbereitende Übungen. Der Anschlag der Töne	2
Der Zungenstoß	4
Kleine Übungsstücke mit Zungenstoß	8
Duette	12
Gestopfte Töne	21
Die Ventiltöne	22
Leichte Volkslieder als Vortragsstudien	24
Die Transposition	28
Tonleitern in Dur und Moll	29
Übungen für Naturhorn in der diatonischen Tonleiter	35
Übungen in den Intervallen	36
Übungen in den chromatischen Intervallen	37
Chromatische Übungen	38
Gebundene Töne	40
Fortsetzung der Duette	42
Die Verzierungen in der Musik	48
Leichte, fortschreitende Übungsstücke	52
Übung zum Aushalten der Töne	60
Übungen in der C-Dur Tonleiter	62
Tonleitern verschiedener Tonarten	64
Gebrochene Akkorde	65
Dreißig Übungsstücke für die Artikulation	67
Das gleichzeitige Hervorbringen doppelter und dreifacher Töne	72
Das Echo	74
Praktische Ratschläge für Orchestermusiker	75
Sechs charakteristische Studien	81
Sechs große Präludien	88
Anhang. Schwierige Orchesterstellen, welche sich in Symphonien und Opern vorfinden	95

CONTENTS	Pag.
3 Designs: The manner of holding the horn	
Preface	
Preparatory Exercises on tone production	2
The Tongue-Stroke	4
Short Exercises on the Tongue-Stroke	8
Duets	12
The "stopped" or closed Notes	21
The tones of the Ventil-horn	22
Easy Popular Airs (Volkslieder) for the development of taste and expression	24
Transposition	28
Major and minor Scales	29
Exercises for Natural horn, on the diatonic scale	35
Exercises on the Intervals	36
Exercises on the chromatic Intervals	37
Exercises on the chromatic scale	38
Slurred Notes	40
Duets	42
The Embellishments in Music	48
Easy and Progressive Exercises	52
Exercise for sustaining the tone	60
Exercises on the scale of C major	62
Scales in different Keys	64
Divided chords	65
Thirty Exercises for Articulation	67
Simultaneous Production of double and triple Tones	72
The Production of the Echo	74
Practical Hints to the Orchestral Artist	75
Six Characteristic Studies	81
Six grand Preludes	88
Supplement. Difficult orchestral passages, to be met with in Symphonies and Operas	95

TABLE	Pag.
3 Figures: La manière de tenir le cor	
Préface	
Premiers exercices pour apprendre à frapper les sons	2
Des coups de langue	4
Petites Études sur les coups de langue	8
Duos	12
Les sons bouchés	21
Les sons produits par les pistons ou cylindres	22
Airs populairs faciles pour former le goût et l'expression	24
De la transposition	28
Gammes majeures et mineures	29
Exercices sur la Gamme diatonique spécialement pour le cor simple	35
Exercices sur les Intervalles	36
Exercices sur les Intervalles chromatiques	37
Exercices sur la Gamme chromatique	38
Des Notes coulées	40
Suite des Duos	42
Les agréments de la musique	48
Études faciles et progressives	52
Étude des sons filés	60
Exercices sur la gamme d'Ut-majeur	62
Gammes en différents tons	64
Accords brisés	65
Trente exercices sur les articulations	67
Des sons doubles et triples que l'on peut produire sur le cor	72
De l'Echo, que l'on peut produire sur le cor	74
Conseils pratiques pour l'artiste de l'orchestre	75
Six Études caractéristiques	81
Six grands Préludes	88
Supplément. Passages difficiles se rencontrant soit dans la Symphonie, soit dans l'Opéra	95

Vorbereitende Übungen

Der Anschlag der Töne

Der Ton ist frei mit der Zunge anzuschlagen, besonders hüte man sich vor dem Aufblasen der Backen.

Preparatory Exercises

On tone production

The tone should be given out freely with the tongue, and without inflating the cheeks.

Premiers Exercices

Pour apprendre à frapper les sons

Attaquez franchement les sons avec la langue, évitez de gonfler les joues.

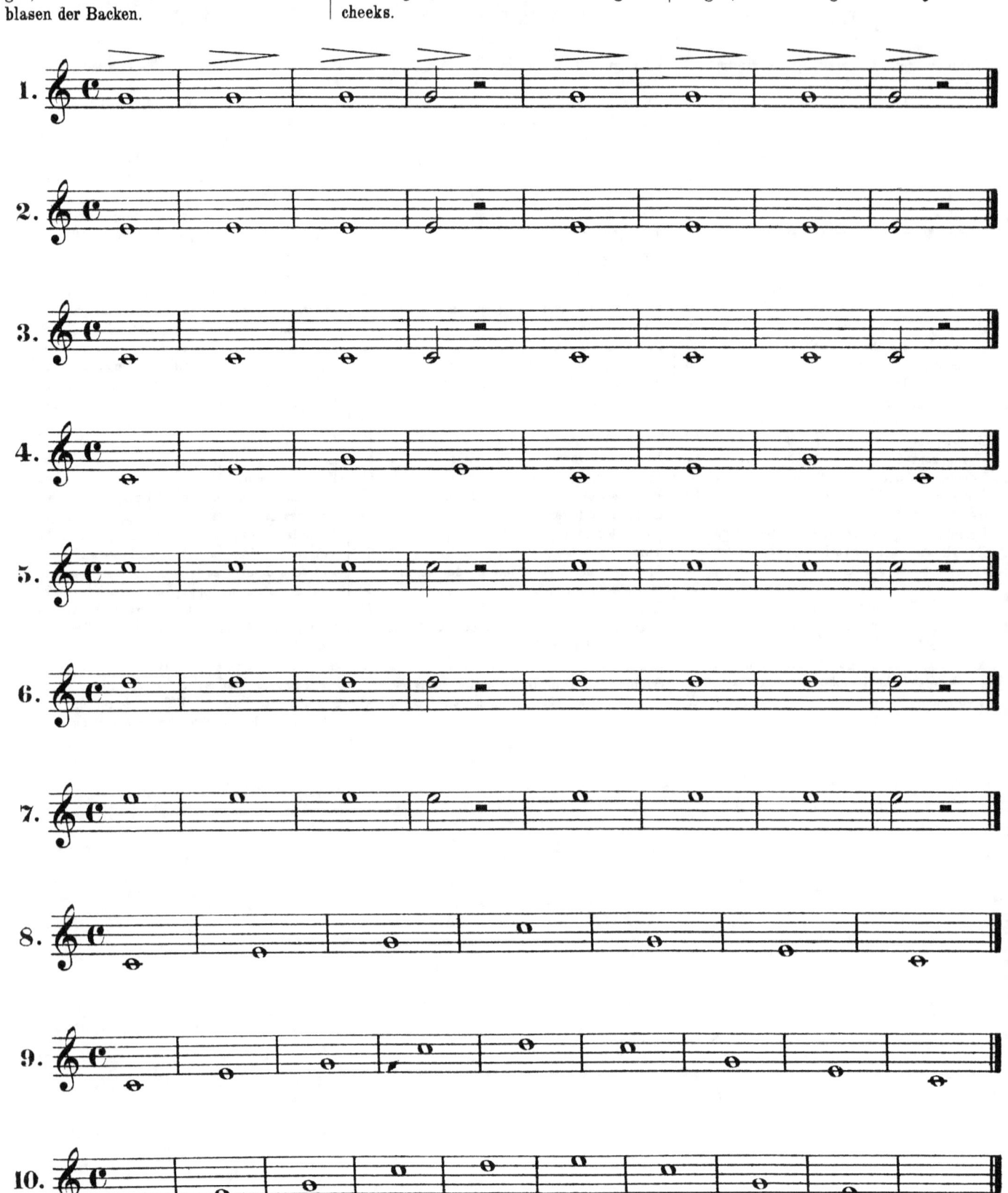

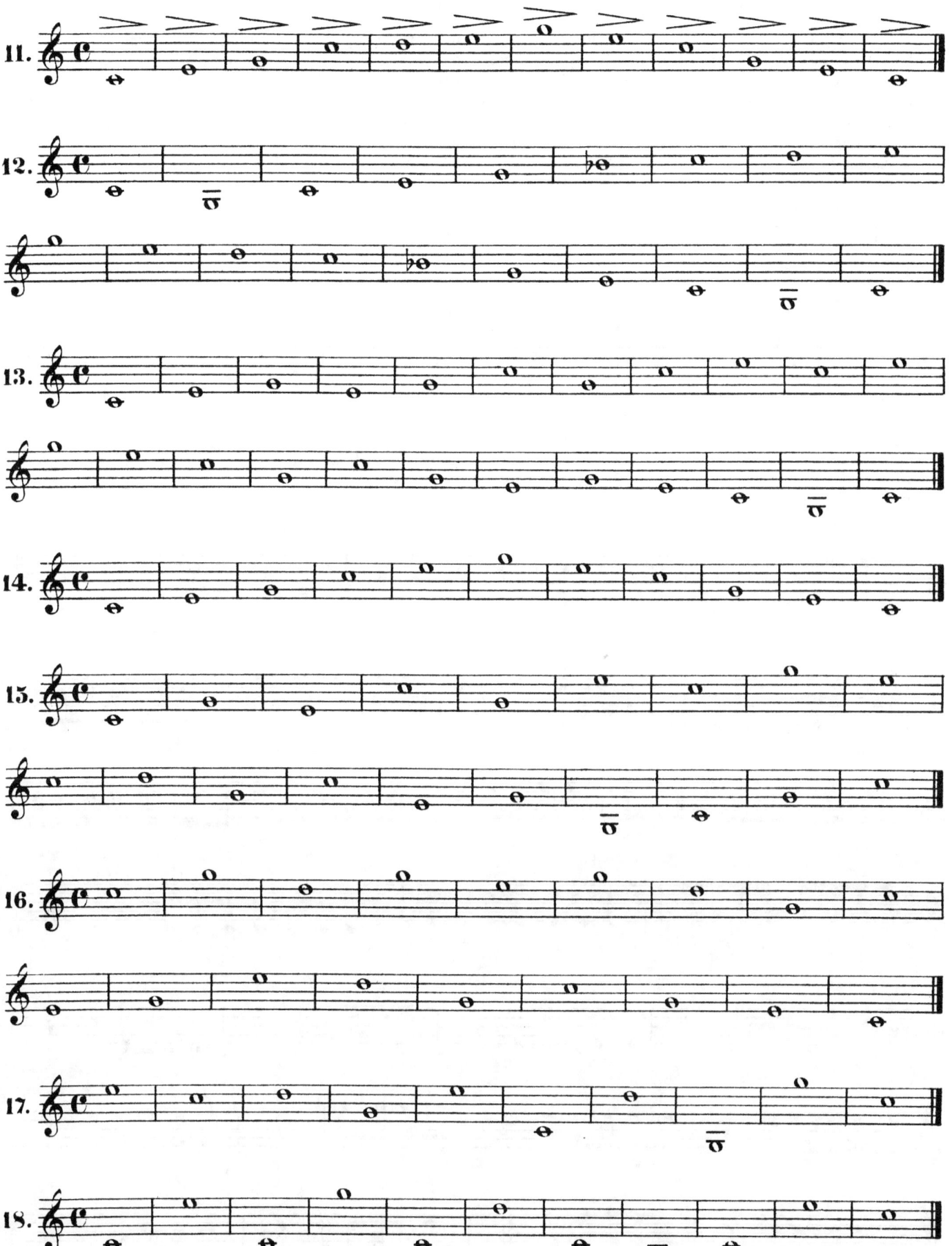

Der Zungenstoß.

Man beachte, daß jede Note mit gleicher Stärke angeblasen und ausgehalten werden muß, um eine vollständige Gleichheit zu erzielen. Man achte ferner auf das freie Anstoßen mit der Zunge, um sich nicht die abscheuliche Gewohnheit anzueignen, die Töne mit der Kehle herauszupressen.

The Tongue-Stroke.

Care must be had to impart to every note the same degree of force, so as to ensure perfect equality. The notes should be given out freely with the tongue only, the pupil being cautioned against contracting the repulsive habit of squeezing out the tone from his throat.

Des coups de Langue.

Il faut avoir soin de donner à chaque note le même degré de force, afin que l'égalité soit parfaite. Que l'attaque des notes soit faite avec la langue, pour ne pas contracter l'habitude monstrueuse de pousser les sons avec le gosier.

Synkopen / Syncopated Notes / Syncopes

NB. Die letzte Hälfte der synkopierten Noten darf nie betont werden. Sollte sich dieser Fehler schon eingeschlichen haben, dann muß er verbessert werden.

Note. The second half of the syncopated notes should never be specially emphasized. Where this fault has been already contracted, it should be corrected.

Nota: Il arrive quelquefois qu'on fait sentir la seconde partie de la syncope, c'est une faute dont il faut se déshabituer:

Bspl: / Ex:

Schlecht. / Bad. / Mauvais.

Gut. / Good. / Bon.

Kleine Übungsstücke mit Zungenstoß | Short Exercises on the Tongue-Stroke | Petites Etudes sur les coups de langue

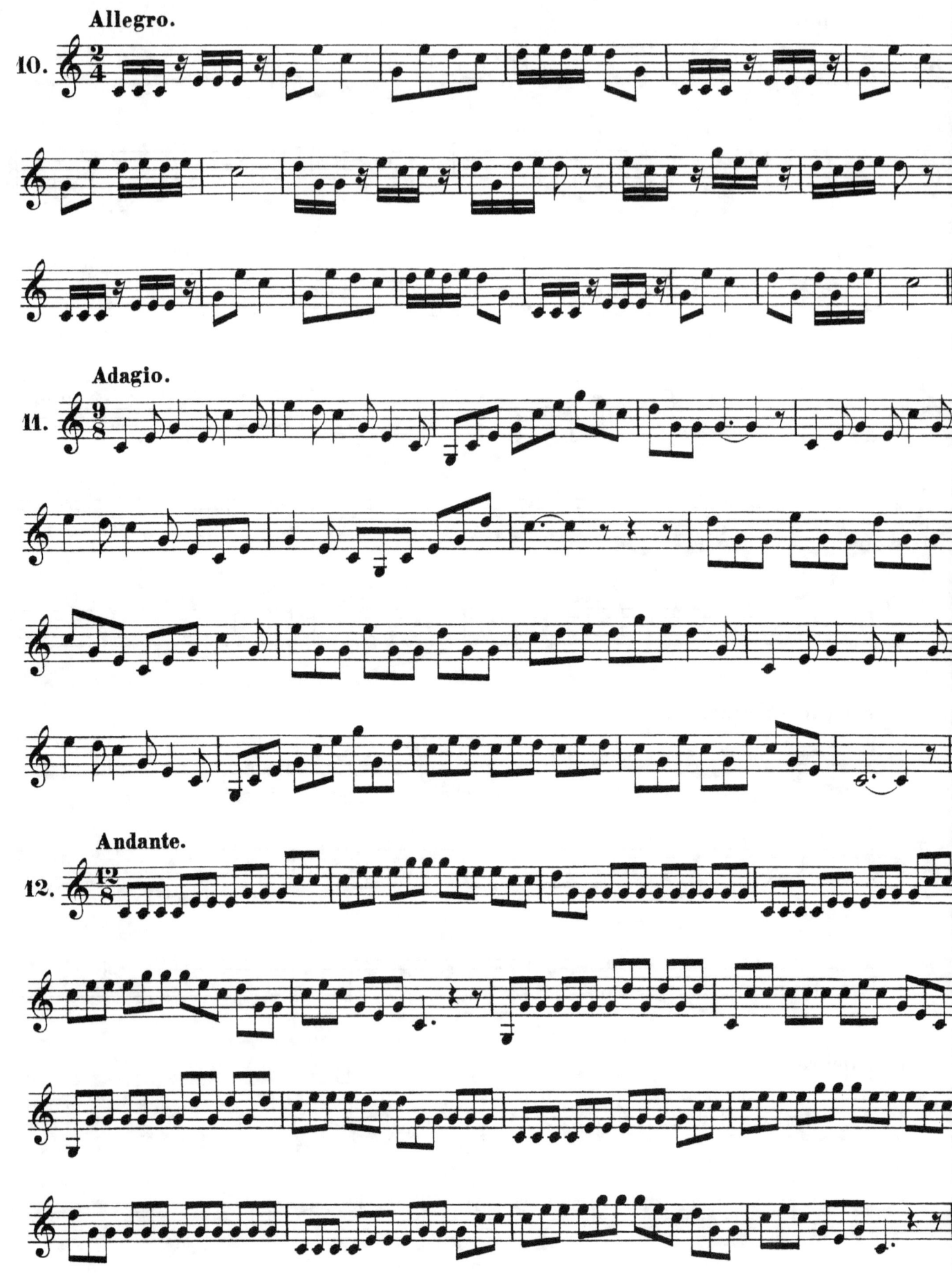

Duette	Duets	Duos
In folgenden Beispielen müssen abwechselnd beide Partien vom Schüler gespielt werden, um sich mit den tiefen Tönen des Instrumentes vertraut zu machen.	In the following exercises the pupil should practise both parts alternately, so as to familiarise himself with the lower as well as the upper notes of his instrument.	Dans les exemples suivants, les élèves joueront alternativement les secondes parties afin de se familiariser avec les sons graves de l'instrument.

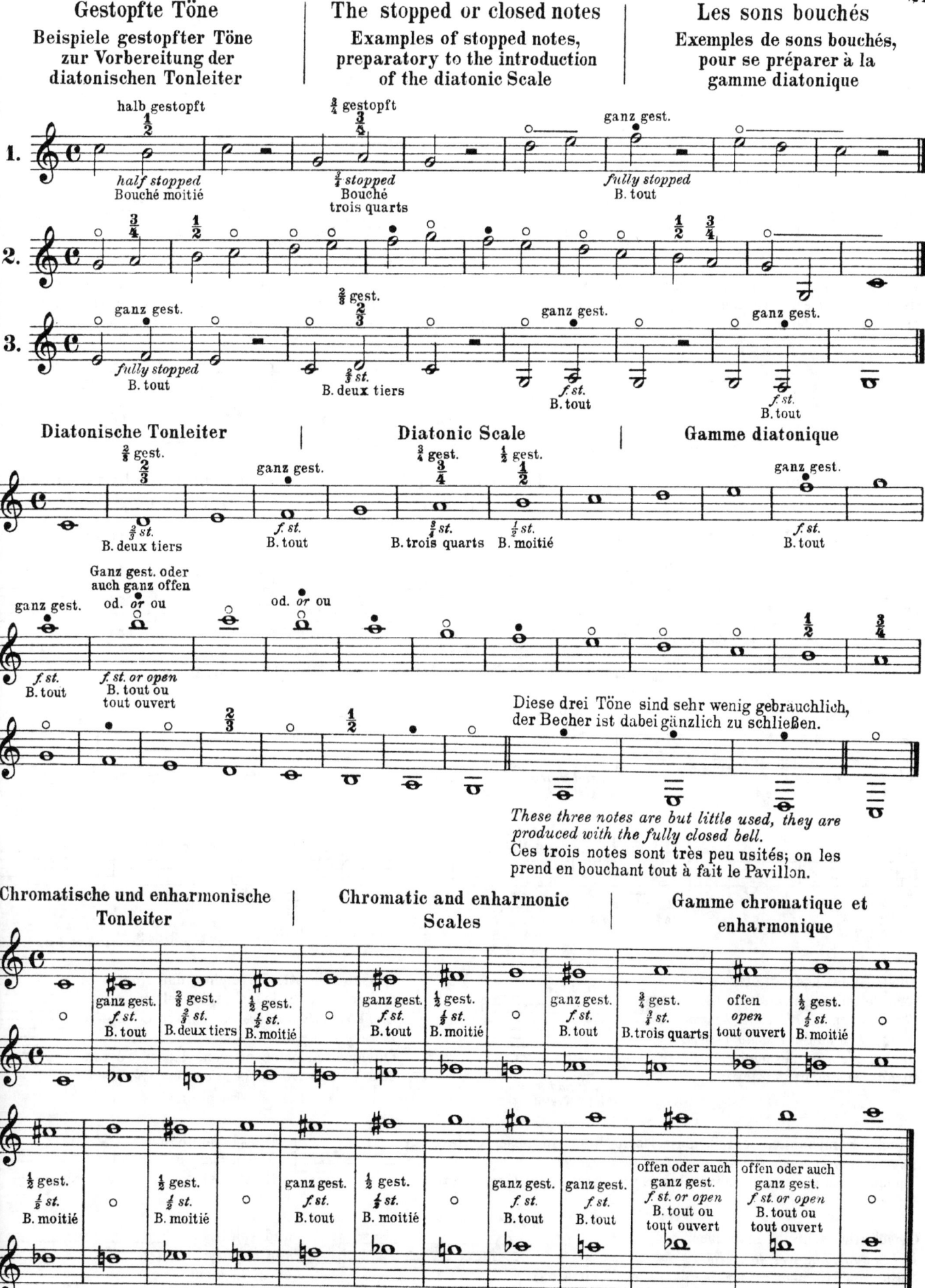

| Beispiele gestopfter Töne, welche sehr wenig gebraucht werden | Examples of stopped notes, which are very little used | Exemple de sons bouchés très peu usités |

ganz gest. / *f. st.* / B. tout   *ganz gest.* / *f. st.* / B. tout   *ganz gest.* / *f. st.* / B. tout   ½ *gest.* / ½ *st.* / B. moitié

| NB: Das *As* (*Gis*) kann man in langsamen Stellen auch offen, vermittelst Anschwellen des Tones, blasen. | Note: The *A flat* (*G sharp*) may also be played open, in slow passages, with gradual swelling of the tone. | Nota: Le *lab* (*sol♯*) de la première octave peut se prendre tout ouvert dans des passages lents, en enflant le son. |

Bspl: / Ex: / Ex: Adagio

| Die Ventiltöne | The Tones of the Ventil-horn | Les sons produits par les pistons ou cylindres |
| Diatonische Tonleiter | Diatonic Scale | Gamme diatonique |

mit herabgedrücktem 1. Ventil / press down 1st Ventil / baissez le 1. Pist. ou Cyl.

1. 2. Ventil od. 3. / 1. 2. Ventil or 3. / baissez les 2 prem. ou le 3. seul

1. Ventil / press down 1. Ventil / baissez le 1. Pist. ou Cyl.

1. 2. od. 3. / 1. 2. or 3. / les 2 prem. ou le 3. seul

1. u. 2. od. 2. od. 3. / 1. and 2. or 2. or 3. / les 2 premiers ou le 2. seul ou le 3. seul

1. 2. od. 2. od. 3. / 1. 2. or 2. or 3. / le 1. 2. ou 2. ou 3.

od. 1. / or 1. / ou 1.

od. 1. / or 1. / ou 1.

1. 2. od. 3. / 1. 2. or 3. / 1. 2. ou 3.

1. / le 1.

1. u. 2. od. 3. / 1. and 2. or 3. / le 1. et 2. ou 3.

2. or 1. 2. or 3. / le 2. ou 1. 2. ou 3.

2. / le 2.

1. u. 2. u. 3. / 1. and 2. and 3. / le 1. et 2. ou 3.

od. 1. 2. 3. / or 1. 2. 3. / ou 1. 2. 3.

1. / le 1.

1. u. 2. od. 3. / 1. and 2. or 3. / le 1. et 2. ou 3.

1. u. 3. od. 1. 2. 3. / 1. and 3. or 1. 2. 3. / le 1. et 3. ou 1. 2. 3.

2.

1. u. 2. od. 3. / 1. and 2. or 3. / le 1. et 2. ou 3.

1. u. 3. od. 1. 2. 3. / 1. and 3. or 1. 2. 3. / le 1. et 3. ou 1. 2. 3.

Auch *Fis* ist noch zu blasen, jedoch selten angewandt:	Einige Künstler erreichen das *Kontra-C*, dieser Fall ist jedoch **sehr selten**.
The *F sharp* may likewise be produced, it is however seldom used:	Some artists achieve the contra C, but it is very exceptional.
Quelque fois on descend encore au *Fa♯* rarement employé:	Quelques artistes peuvent descendre jusqu'à l'Ut grave, mais le cas est très rare.

1. 2. u. 3. / 1. 2. and 3. / les 1. 2. et 3.

Manche Komponisten schreiben die Hornstimme in dieser Oktave:
Some composers note the horn part in this octave:
Quelques compositeurs écrivent les parties graves du Cor à cette octave:

Wirklicher Klang:
Notes actually produced:
Effet réel:

Gewöhnlich schreibt man aber:
It is usual, however, to write:
Mais généralement ce dernier passage s'écrit ainsi:

und spielt:
and to play:
et on l'exécute:

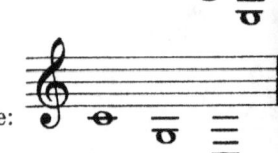

| Chromatische und enharmonische Tonleiter | Chromatic and enharmonic Scales | Gamme chromatique et enharmonique |

Folgende Töne werden wenig gebraucht und sind übrigens fast unmöglich hervorzubringen:
The following, little used, tones are well-nigh impracticable:
Les Notes suivantes sont peu usitées, et de plus d'une exécution presque impossible:

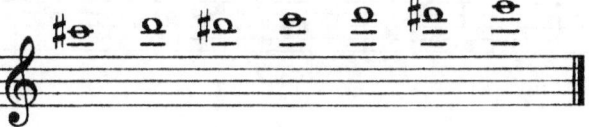

Leichte Volkslieder als Vortragsstudien

Das Studium der hier folgenden Volkslieder hat den Zweck, das musikalische Vortragsgefühl des angehenden Hornisten zu erwekken und ihn zum täglichen fleißigen Blasen zu ermuntern.

Ich wiederhole hier nochmals die Mahnung, daß der Schüler, um der Ermüdung und Erschlaffung der Lippen vorzubeugen, jedesmal nur wenig aber öfters blasen soll. Diese Regel ist für alle Studien anwendbar, denn nur durch ein einsichtsvoll eingeteiltes Studium wird man den Lippen die nötige Kraft und Ausdauer verschaffen können, welche zum Vortrag eines Adagio, eines Cantabile oder eines Andante erforderlich ist.

Easy Popular Airs (Volkslieder) for the development of taste and expression

The popular airs here given are intended to awaken musical feeling in the pupil and to encourage him in his daily practices.

I once more revert to the previously made observation that, in order to avoid fatiguing the lips, practices should be of short duration, at one time, but frequent. This maxim is applicable to all the different studies, for it is only by gradual and judiciously timed practice that the lips will attain the firmness and strength requisite for the performance of an Adagio, a Cantabile, or an Andante.

Airs populairs faciles pour former le goût et l'expression

L'étude des airs populaires suivants a pour but d'éveiller le goût musical de l'élève et de le stimuler à l'étude journalière du cor. Je répète ici encore une fois la recommandation que pour éviter la fatigue des lèvres il faut jouer peu à la fois mais souvent. Cette règle s'applique à toutes les études, car ce n'est que par un travail intelligent et bien gradué que l'on acquerra la force indispensable de lèvres pour soutenir un Adagio, un Cantabile ou un Andante.

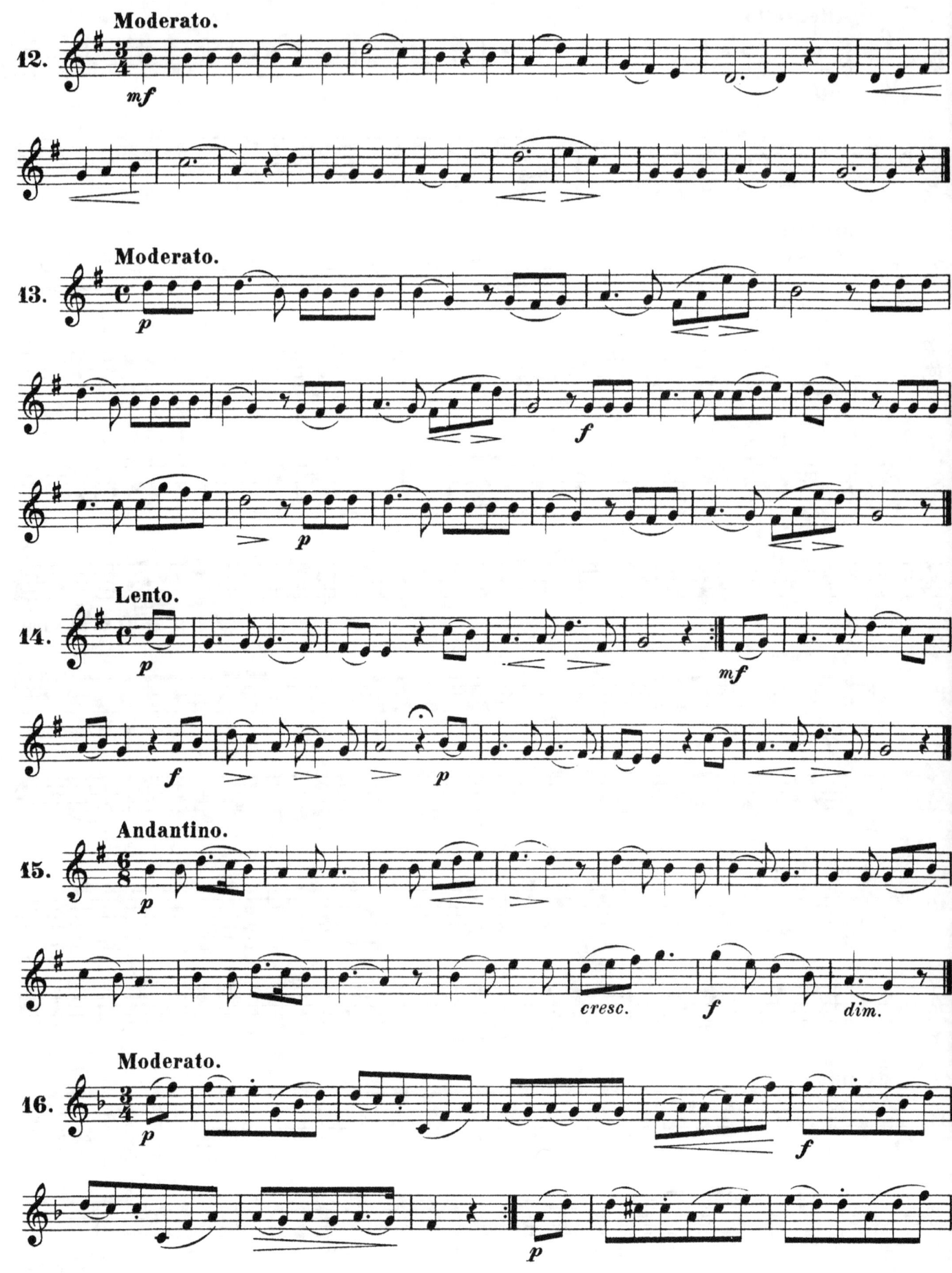

Die Transposition | Transposition | De la transposition

Das Ventilhorn ist unumgänglich im modernen Orchester notwendig. Ungeachtet daß die Mehrzahl unserer Komponisten die Gewohnheit hat, in ihren Partituren die Veränderungen der Tonarten anzuzeigen: Horn in F, in Es, in D, in C, in G, u.s.w., ziehen die meisten Künstler doch vor, sich nicht an das jeden Augenblick wiederkehrende Wechseln der Tonart vermittels Bogenwechsels zu halten. Sie spielen vielmehr fast immer auf F-Horn, indem sie nach der vorgeschriebenen Tonart bald eine Sekunde, eine Terz, eine Quarte und eine Quinte höher oder tiefer transponieren. Die drei Ventile sind hierbei von großem Nutzen und erleichtern das Spielen schwieriger Stellen.

The Ventil Horn is indispensable in the modern orchestra. Although in the majority of cases composers will indicate the changes of key in their scores —as, "horn in F, in E flat, in D, in C, in G, etc.- yet most executants, instead of having to change crooks every instant, prefer to play almost invariably on the F horn, transposing by a second, third, fourth, or fifth higher or lower, in accordance with the key actually prescribed. For this purpose, the three valves or ventils are of the greatest service and facilitate in a peculiar manner the rendering of complicated passages.

Le Cor à pistons ou à cylindres est indispensable pour l'orchestre moderne. Quoique la plupart de nos compositeurs aient coutume d'indiquer dans leurs partitions les changements de tons, tels que: en Fa, en Mi♭, en Ré♮, en Ut, en Sol, etc. etc. la pluralité des artistes préfèrent ne pas s'astreindre à changer de ton de rechange à chaque instant, et par conséquent, jouent presque toujours sur le ton de Fa en transposant soit une seconde, une tierce, une quarte, une quinte plus haute ou plus basse, selon le ton indiqué. Les 3 pistons sont pour cela d'une grande utilité et facilitent singulièrement les passages compliqués.

Bspl: Horn in Es
Exple: Horn in E flat
Ex: Cor en Mi♭

Wird auf F-Horn durch das Niederdrücken des ersten Ventiles gespielt. | Played on the F horn, while pressing down the first ventil. | Ce passage peut s'exécuter sur le ton de Fa, en baissant le I⁰ piston ou cylindre.

Ausführung:
Effect:
Effet:

Dies ist die Transposition um einen ganzen Ton tiefer. | Here the transposition is an entire tone lower. | C'est ce que l'on appelle transposer un ton plus bas.

Horn in E
Horn in E
Cor en Mi♮

Vorstehendes Beispiel auf F-Horn zu spielen vermittelst des zweiten Ventiles; Transposition um einen halben Ton tiefer. | The above example to be played on the F horn, with the second ventil, thereby transposing half a tone lower. | Le passage précédent peut s'exécuter sur le ton de Fa, en baissant le II⁰ pist. ou cyl., c'est ce que l'on appelle transposer un demi-ton plus bas.

Vermittelst des 2ten Ventiles: Ausführung:
With the 2d ventil: Effect:
Baissant le II de pist. ou cyl: Effet:

Horn in D
Horn in D
Cor en Ré♮

Auf F-Horn: mit dem dritten Ventile. Für diese Stelle könnte man sich auch noch der beiden ersten Ventile bedienen. | On the F horn, with the third ventil. For this passage, however, the two other ventils might be used to the same purpose. | Praticable sur le ton de Fa en baissant le III ème pist. ou cyl. On pourrait encore se servir des deux premiers pist. ou cyl.

Ausführung:
Effect:
Effet:

| Wenn die Stellen für Horn in *G*, in *As*, in *A*, für hoch *B*-und *H-Horn* geschrieben sind, tut man besser, sich der entsprechenden Bogen zu bedienen. Die Transposition wird zu schwierig durch die hohe Lage der Töne. Folgende Stelle für *G-Horn*: | In the case of passages written for horn in *G*, *A flat*, *A*, for *B flat* and *B* (high) it is advisable to make use of the respective crooks, transposition being rendered difficult on account of the high pitch of the notes. The following passage for the *G horn*. | Si les passages sont écrits pour les tons de *Sol*, *Lab*, *La♮*, *Si♭* ou *Si♮* haut, on fera bien de se servir des tons de rechange indiqués. La transposition devient difficile à cause de l'élévation du ton. Ainsi le passage suivant sur le *ton de Sol*: |

| auf *F-Horn* transponiert, ist schon schwer auszuführen. Aus diesem Grunde ist der *G-Bogen* vorzuziehen. | If transposed on the *F horn* already presents difficulties in execution. The *G* crook is therefore preferably used. | Transposé avec le ton de *Fa*, est d'une execution déjà plus difficile, il est donc préférable de se servir du ton de *Sol*. |

| Folgende Stelle für *A-Horn*: | Similarly in the passage for *A horn* | Il en est de même pour le ton de *La♮* |

| auf *F-Horn* transponiert, ist fast unmöglich zu blasen. | transposed on the *F horn* it is almost impracticable. | transposé avec le ton de *Fa* devient presque impossible. |

| Auf jedem Bogen transponiert man nun in der angegebenen Weise vermittelst der Ventile, und erzielt dadurch eine Menge verschiedener Tonarten. Die Transposition erlernt sich nicht in einem Tage. Um ihrer vollständig Herr zu werden, bedarf es einer großen Übung. Aus diesem Grunde möchte ich den Herren Lehrern anraten, ihre Schüler frühzeitig zu diesem Studium anzuhalten, wie auch dieselben auf allen Bogen spielen zu lassen, damit das Gehör der Schüler geübt wird, und sie sich an die verschiedenen Klangarten ihres Instrumentes gewöhnen. Wer diese Kunst theoretisch und praktisch zu erlernen wünscht, dem empfehle ich meine „Praktische Anweisung zum Transponieren". (Verlag von L. Oertel, in Hannover) | With every crook transposition is effected by means of the three ventils, and a great number of different keys may thereby be commanded. The art of transposing is, however, not acquired in a day. Much practice and diligent application will be required before completely mastering it. I would therefore recommend teachers to insist upon their pupils applying themselves early to this study and also upon their playing upon all the crooks, so as to train the ear and accustom it to the qualities peculiar to the different tonalities. Pupils desirous of studying the subject thoroughly, both theoretically and practically, may be referred to my "Practical Directions for Transposing." (Hanover: L. Oertel.) | Sur chaque ton de rechange on peut transposer au moyen des 3 pist. ou cyl. ce qui donne une multitude de tons différents. La transposition ne s'apprend pas d'un seul jour, il faut une longue pratique pour s'en rendre maître. Je conseille donc à MM. les Professeurs de commencer de bonne heure à appliquer leurs élèves à cette étude, ainsi que de les faire jouer sur tous les tons de rechange, afin d'exercer leur oreille à s'habituer à ces différentes tonalités. A l'élève qui désire apprendre à fond l'art de transposer, je lui recommande mon «Traité pratique pour la Transposition» (Hanovre, chez L. Oertel) |

Tonleitern in Dur und Moll | Major and minor scales | Gammes majeures et mineures

| Alltägliches fleißiges Studieren nachfolgender Tonleitern ist unentbehrlich, um einen schönen, reinen Ton zu erzielen. | Diligent daily practice of the subjoined scales will be absolutely necessary for the purpose of acquiring a good and pure tone. | L'Etude journalière des gammes suivantes est indispensable pour acquérir une belle qualité de son. |

C-dur— C major— Ut-majeur
Tempo moderato

Der Schüler / *Pupil* / L'Elève
Der Lehrer / *Teacher* / Le Professeur

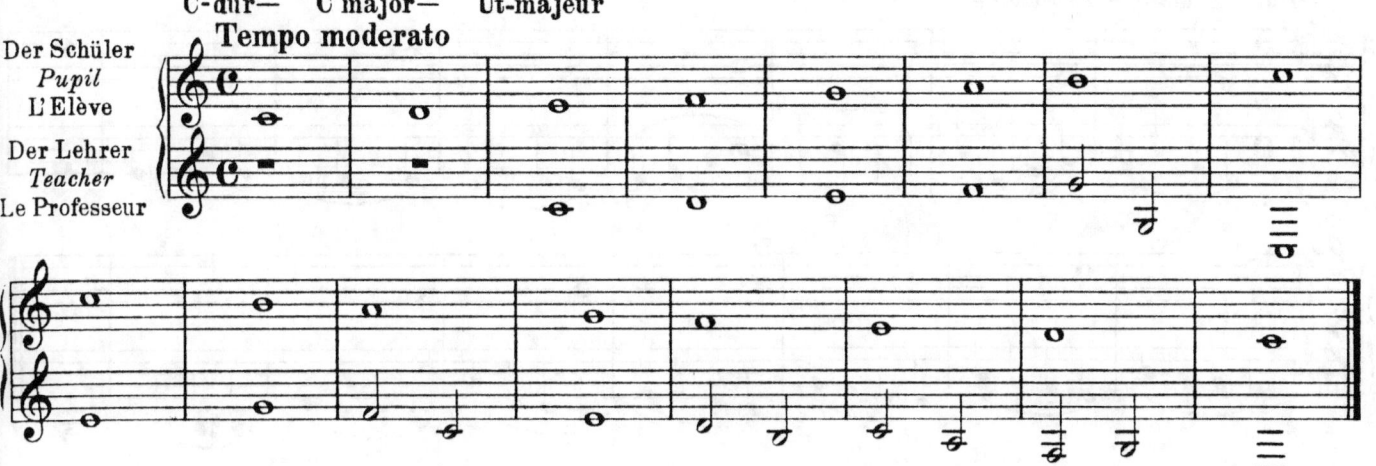

32

Cis-moll - C sharp minor - Do#-mineur

F-Dur - F major - Fa-majeur

D-moll - D minor - Ré♮-mineur

34

As-Dur- A flat major- La♭-majeur

F-moll- F minor- Fa-mineur

Chromatische Tonleiter | Chromatic Scale | Gamme chromatique

Übungen für Naturhorn in der diatonischen Tonleiter | Exercises for Natural Horn, on the diatonic Scale | Exercices sur la Gamme diatonique, spécialement pour le cor simple

Übungen in den Intervallen | Exercises on the Intervals | Exercices sur les Intervalles

Sekunden / Seconds / Secondes

Terzen / Thirds / Tierces

Quarten / Fourths / Quartes

Quinten / Fifths / Quintes

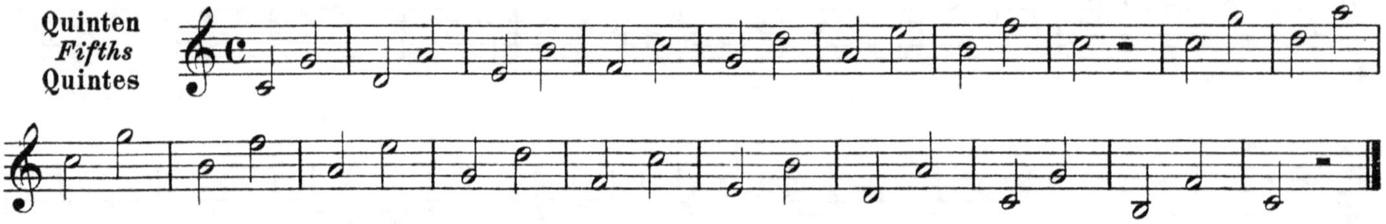

Sexten / Sixths / Sixtes

Septimen / Sevenths / Septièmes

Chromatische Übungen | Exercises on the chromatic Scale | Exercices sur la Gamme chromatique

Gebundene Töne

Um die Töne auf- oder absteigend zu binden, gleitet man ohne Zungenstoß von dem ersten Ton nach dem zweiten, zu gleicher Zeit einen leisen Lippendruck nach dem zweiten Ton hin gebend.

Slurred Notes

In the rendering of slurred notes, ascending or descending, the legato is produced by gliding from one note on to the other, with a slight pressure of the lips, but without tongue-stroke.

Des Notes coulées

Pour faire les coulées, il faut glisser et appuyer les lèvres sur la note suivante, sans donner de coup de langue, soit en montant, soit en descendant.

Fortsetzung der Duette | Duets | Suite des Duos

aus „Titus" von Mozart
from "La Clemenza di Tito," Mozart
tiré de «Titus» de Mozart

Als weitere Fortsetzung der Duette, deren Studium ebenso angenehm als nützlich ist, wähle man meine „30 leichte Duette in fortschreitender Folge für 2 Waldhörner" und auf diese meine „20 Duos progressivs für 2 Waldhörner". (Beide Werke bei L. Oertel in Hannover erschienen.) Auch die Duette von Gallay, Niesle, Grimm, Schunke, Dauprat, sowie die von vielen andern ausgezeichneten Künstlern komponierten Stücke sind zum Studium sehr empfehlenswert. Die Wahl bleibe dem Lehrer überlassen, welcher sich nach den Kräften und Fähigkeiten seiner Schüler richten wird. Bei hinreichender Schülerzahl möchte ich auch Ensemblestücke empfehlen, Horntrios oder Hornquartette. Für Horntrios gibt es keine bessere und lusterregendere als meine „30 leichte Unterhaltungsstücke für 3 Waldhörner" (Verlag von L. Oertel in Hannover.) Nichts von dem darf überhaupt übergangen werden, was den guten Geschmack und Stil des Schülers bildet.

As a further continuation of the duets, the study whereof is at once pleasing and profitable, my "Thirty easy and progressive Duets for two horns", and after these, the "Twenty progressive Duets for two horns" (both published by L. Oertel, Hanover) will prove useful. The duets by Gallay, Niesle, Grimm, Schunke, Dauprat, and many other distinguished professors, are likewise to be highly recommended; it being left to the teacher to select from them with a view to the respective capacities of his pupils. Where there is a sufficient number of pupils available, I would also advise the study of trios and quartets for horns. As regards the former, my "Thirty easy Trios" for three horns (Hanover: L. Oertel) will be found in every way suitable for the purpose. No useful adjunct, in fine, for stimulating the zeal and forming the taste of pupils should be disregarded.

Pour continuer les Duos, dont l'exercice est aussi agréable qu'utile, il faut prendre mes „30 Duos faciles et progressifs" pour 2 Cors, et après ceux-ci mes „20 Duos progressifs pour 2 Cors". (Les deux oeuvres ont parues chez L. Oertel, à Hanovre.) Les Duos de Gallay, Niesle, Grimm, Schunke, Dauprat, et de tant d'autres artistes distingués, selon le choix de M. M. les Professeurs, suivant les forces et les aptitudes de leurs élèves, sont également très recommandables. S'il y a un nombre d'élèves suffisant, je recommanderai aussi la musique d'ensemble, soit Trios, Quatuors de Cors. Pour les Trios, on devra prendre mes „30 Trios faciles et agréables" pour 3 Cors. (Chez L. Oertel, à Hanovre.) Il ne faut rien négliger de ce qui peut former le goût et le style de l'élève.

Die Verzierungen in der Musik | The embellishments in music | Les agréments de la musique

Nachstehendes bietet einen kurzgefaßten Überblick über diejenigen Verzierungen der Musik, welche auf dem Horn die gebräuchlichsten sind.

The following is a brief summary of the various graces most in use on the horn.

Je donne ici un petit aperçu des divers agréments de la musique qui sont les plus usités sur le cor.

Der Triller | The Shake | Du Trille

Der Triller, nicht zutreffend auch Cadenz genannt, besteht aus einer kleinen, über oder unter der trillernden Hauptnote gesetzten Note welche mit jener abwechselnd angeschlagen wird.

Zur Erzielung des Trillers auf dem Horne, muß man auf- und absteigende beide Noten langsam in einander ziehen. Nach erlangtem gleichmäßigem Anschlage beider Töne steigere man allmählig die Geschwindigkeit bis zur größtmöglichen Schnelligkeit. Es ist die Sache des Lehrers den Schüler bei dieser Übung zu leiten, er richte sich nach den mehr oder weniger entwickelten, musikalischen Anlagen desselben.

The shake, sometimes incorrectly called the cadence, consists (in notation) of a small note placed either above or below the one on which the shake is to be given, and which is alternately sounded with it.

In order to acquire the shake on the horn, the principal note and its subsidiary should be, at first, slowly glided one into the other, both in ascending and descending. When this has been perfectly accomplished, in an absolutely even manner, the speed may be gradually increased until the greatest possible rapidity has been reached. It must be left to the teacher, to guide the pupil in this study in accordance with the more or less developed musical capacities of the latter.

Le trille, qu'on appelle improprement Cadence, est composé d'une petite note placée au-dessus ou au dessous de la note que l'on doit triller ou cadencer, et que l'on articule alternativement avec cette même note.

Pour faire le trille sur le cor, il faut couler lentement les deux notes en montant et en descendant. Lorsque l'on sera parvenu à les faire d'une manière égale, on les fera plus vite, par gradations jusqu'au dernier degré de vitesse. C'est au professeur qu'appartient le droit de guider son élève suivant les dispositions musicales plus ou moins développées de ce dernier.

Sehr langsam und mit vollständiger Gleichheit der Töne. | Very slowly and with perfect evenness of tone. | Très lent, et d'une parfaite égalité dans le son.

Art und Weise den Triller zu üben: | The way to practise the shake: | Manière d'étudier le trille:

Sehr langsam, nach und nach immer schneller. | Very slowly, with gradually increasing speed. | Très lent d'abord en augmentant peu à peu de vitesse.

Um eine tadellose Ausführung des Trillers zu erzielen, übe man ihn jeden Tag mit Ausdauer.

For the acquisition of a faultless shake, it is necessary to practise it diligently and perseveringly every day.

Si l'on veut parvenir à le faire comme il faut, c'est chaque jour qu'il faut l'étudier et y mettre de la persévérance.

Unter den verschiedenen Manieren den Triller anzufangen oder zu endigen, sind die drei nachstehenden Arten die gebräuchlichsten:

The following three examples represent the most usual ways of commencing and concluding the shake.

Il y a plusieurs manières de commencer et de terminer le trille, en voici quelques spécimens les plus usités:

Bspl. Bezeichnung: | Exple. Notation: | Ex. Indication:

Auf andere Art geschrieben: | Another manner of noting it: | Autre manière de les écrire:

Bei folgenden Trillern darf man die Hand im Becher nicht bewegen, selbst nicht bei den Naturtönen. Der Becher bleibt demnach offen. Bei einiger Übung sprechen diese Töne doch an. Den Nachschlag macht man natürlich mit der Hand.

In the following examples of the shake, the hand must not be inserted in the bell, not even for the natural tones, or "harmonics". The bell, therefore remains open, and only for the termination, or "turn", of the shake the hand is employed.

Pour les trilles suivants, il ne faut pas boucher la deuxième note excepté pour la terminaison du trille, en conséquence le pavillon reste ouvert:

| Bei den Trillern auf folgenden Noten bleibt alles gestopft, man öffnet die Hand nur für die Nachschläge: | In the subjoined shake exercises, all the notes are "stopped", and the hand is only opened for the terminations or "turns": | Les trilles qui suivent se font sans déranger la main, qui ne s'ouvre que pour les terminaisons: |

| Auch auf dem Ventilhorn ist es gut, diese Triller auf dieselbe Weise d. h. vermittelst der Hand im Becher auszuführen. Es versteht sich von selbst, daß man diese Triller mit ziemlicher Geschwindigkeit ausführen muß, um ein befriedigendes Resultat zu erzielen. Das Studium dieser Triller bietet große Schwierigkeiten; jedoch bei täglich wiederholter ausdauernder Übung überwindet man auch diese. | It is advisable to execute the shake in the same way on the Ventil horn, i. e. with the hand in the bell. It is scarcely necessary to add that the shakes must be executed with some rapidity if a satisfactory result is to be attained. The study of these different shakes presents great difficulties, which can be surmounted only by persevering daily practice. | Pour le cor chromatique il est bon d'exécuter les trilles de la même manière, c'est à dire en se servant de la main. Il va sans dire que ces trilles devront être attaqués avec vitesse, si l'on veut obtenir un résultat satisfaisant. L'étude de ces trilles offre de grandes difficultés, mais on parviendra à les vaincre avec un travail journalier et opiniâtre. |

| Der Pralltriller ist eine Unterart des Trillers von kurzer Dauer ohne Vor- und Nachschlag. | The Prall-triller or Passing shake is a short shake, without either preparatory note, or "turns". | Le Petit trille, fort court, sans préparation attaqué subitement et interrompu presque aussitôt. |

| Die Triller, welche in einem schnellen Tempo auszuführen sind, bedürfen keines Nachschlages. | Successive shakes, which are to be played in rapid tempo, require no "turns". | Les Trilles exécutés dans un mouvement rapide n'ont pas besoin de terminaison. |

| Der Doppelschlag oder Mordent besteht aus vier kleinen Noten, eine große, kleine oder verminderte Terz, je nach der Tonart, in der er steht, bildend. | The Mordent is a grace composed of four small notes, forming a major, minor, or diminished third, according to the key in which it occurs. | Le Grupetto (petit groupe), est composé de quatre petites notes, et alors il peut faire tierce majeure, mineure ou diminuée, selon le mode et le degré de la gamme sur lequel il se trouve. |

Durch gutgewählte Anwendung dieser Verzierungen, durch Nüancierung und Betonung gibt man sowohl getragenen als lebhaften Stellen Manigfaltigkeit, auf diese Weise die einfachsten Passagen verschönernd und ihnen Färbung, Charakter, Leben gebend.

Much variety may be imparted to different passages by the judicious use of the above graces, and the most simple passages may, in thus giving them added colour, character and animation, be greatly embellished thereby.

C'est par l'emploi bien dirigé de ces divers agréments, ainsi que par les nuances et les articulations que l'on répand de la variété dans le chant et dans les traits; c'est ainsi que l'on embellit les choses les plus simples, qu'on leur donne de la couleur, du caractère, et de la vie.

Leichte, fortschreitende Übungsstücke

Die Nachteile welche für den Schüler aus der Einförmigkeit der Übungen entspringen, nötigen mich, um deren Leere abzuschwächen, diesen Übungsstücken hier ihren Platz anzuweisen; gewissermaßen als Erholung, mit dem Endzwecke der Bildung des guten Geschmackes des Schülers. Sehr wesentlich ist das gleichzeitige Studium der Tonleitern mit der bezeichneten Betonung. Das öftere Spielen sämtlicher Tonleitern ist von der allergrößten Wichtigkeit; es verschafft dem Schüler Geschmeidigkeit und Festigkeit der Lippen, Gewandheit und Fertigkeit der Hand, unentbehrliche Eigenschaften zur Erlangung vollkommener Meisterschaft.

So auch empfehle ich noch tagtägliches Aushalten der Töne, worin das einzige und unfehlbare Mittel zur Erlangung eines schönen Tones besteht, ohne welchen das Horn, seines eigenartigen Charakters beraubt, der Trompete oder der Posaune ähnlich klingt.

Easy and progressive Exercises

I have thought it advisable, in this place, to introduce the following exercises, for the purpose of counteracting the feeling of monotony which the purely didactic process is otherwise apt to arouse in the pupil. They will serve by way of recreation and will contribute towards the improvement of his taste. Nevertheless, it is very important that he should, at the same time, continue practising the scales, with the proper accentuation, as indicated. This practice is of the greater importance, since upon it will depend, in a great measure, the development of the requisite agility and firmness of the lips and the expertness of the hand; qualities which are altogether indispensable in the acquisition of a perfect execution.

In the same way, I likewise recommend the daily practice of sustained tones, wherein consists the only means of obtaining a good quality of tone, without which the horn is deprived of its individual character and approaches more nearly to that of the trumpet or the trombone.

Etudes faciles et progressives

Les inconvénients qui résultent pour l'élève de la sécheresse des leçons, m'obligent, pour en atténuer l'aridité, à placer ici ces études, comme une simple récréation ayant pour but de stimuler le goût de l'élève. Il est très essentiel que l'élève étudie en même temps toutes les gammes avec les articulations indiquées. Cette étude est de la plus grande importance, attendu qu'elle donne aux lèvres et à la main, l'agilité et la souplesse, deux qualités indispensables pour arriver à l'obtention d'une parfaite exécution.

Je recommanderai aussi de faire journellement l'étude des sons filés, seul moyen d'obtenir une belle qualité de son, sans laquelle le Cor se rapproche de la Trompette ou du Trombone.

Moderato.
Gut abstoßen
Distinctly separated
Bien détaché
15.
f

Adagio espressivo.
16.
p
mf
cresc.
f
rit.

Adagio espressivo.
17.
p
cresc.
f
f
rit.

Andante cantabile.
18.
p

64

Tonleitern verschiedener Tonarten	Scales in different Keys	Gammes en différents Tons
Ich lasse hier zum praktischen Studium nur die auf dem Horne gebräuchlichsten Tonleitern folgen.	Only the scales most usually employed in hornplaying are here given.	Je ne donne ici pour étudier aux élèves que les gammes les plus usitées sur le Cor.

Gebrochene Akkorde

Folgende Übungsstücke werden den Schüler daran gewöhnen, von einem tiefen nach einem hohen Tone, und umgekehrt zu springen. Der Spieler kann die Artikulation in den ersten zwölf Übungsstücken nach seiner Fantasie variieren, jedoch nur erst dann, wenn er dieselben so studiert haben wird, wie sie stehen. Ferner empfehle ich dem Ausführenden, folgende Stücke auch mit heruntergedrücktem 1ten Ventile, dann mit dem 2ten, und zuletzt mit dem 3ten Ventile zu studieren; er wird durch ein solches Studium große Abwechslung der Klangfarbe und große Fertigkeit erzielen.

Divided chords

The following exercises will accustom the pupil to the passing from a low to a high note, and vice versa. The executant may be permitted to vary at his pleasure the accentuation of the first twelve exercises, but only after having studied them as they are written. I likewise recommend the player to practise the subjoined pieces alternately with the first, second and third ventil, as by so doing he will obtain great variety of tone-colour, as well as great dexterity in execution.

Accords Brisés

Les exercices suivants consistent à habituer l'élève à passer d'un ton grave, à un ton aigu, et réciproquement. Il sera loisible à l'exécutant de varier à sa fantaisie l'articulation des douze premières études qui suivent, mais ce ne sera que lorsqu'il les aura travaillées telles qu'elles sont écrites. De même que je recommande aussi à l'exécutant de les étudier sur le I? piston ou cylindre, ensuite sur le IIème et puis sur le IIIème; il obtiendra par là une très grande variété de tons et une très grande facilité d'exécution.

| Dreißig Übungsstücke für die Artikulation | Thirty Exercises for Articulation | Trente exercices sur les articulations |

Das gleichzeitige Hervorbringen doppelter und dreifacher Töne	Simultaneous Production of double and triple Tones	Des sons doubles et triples que l'on peut produire sur le Cor
Im Jahre 1843 fesselte der gefeierte Horn-Virtuose und Komponist Vivier (Eugène) die öffentliche Aufmerksamkeit durch die gemachte Entdeckung eines akustischen Phänomens, dessen Entstehung noch nicht genügend erklärt war. Dieses Phänomen besteht in der gleichzeitigen Hervorbringung mehrerer Töne in der Röhre, welche einen Dreiklang bilden (Übersetzung der sich in Band 8, Seite 370 befindenden Erwähnung in Fétis Universal-Biographie der Musiker.) Nichts leichter zu erklären als das. Zuerst verdient erwähnt zu werden, daß diese Entdeckung nicht Herrn Vivier zugeschrieben werden kann. Das Phänomen war schon C. M. von Weber bekannt, der es in seinem Concertino für Horn und Orchester angewandt hat, dann hatte schon lange Zeit vorher, ehe Vivier mit seiner, für sich in Anspruch genommenen Entdeckung Parade machte, der berühmte Hornist Dauprat den Mechanismus des Phänomens in seiner großen Hornschule erklärt. Zu gleicher Zeit wo man einen Ton mit der Zunge oder den Lippen hervorbringt, kann man einen andern Ton singen, ganz gleich ob höher oder tiefer als der gespielte Ton. Schlägt man z. B. das *C* mit der Zunge an, und singt das eine Terz höher liegende *E* dazu, so kann man selbst chromatisch eine Kette aufsteigender Dreiklänge bilden:	In the year 1843, the celebrated horn virtuoso and composer, Eugène Vivier, created much public interest by the discovery of an acoustic phenomenon, a satisfactory explanation of which was not forthcoming. It consisted in the simultaneous production of several tones in the tube of the horn, forming a consonance or common chord, (see Fétis, Biographie universelle des Musiciens, vol. 8, page 370). The explanation is simple enough. In the first place, the discovery of the phenomenon in question was not Vivier's, it being already well known to C. M. von Weber, who has made use of it in his Concertino for horn and orchestra. Moreover, the famous hornist Dauprat explains the mechanical process, by which this effect is produced, in his great Method for the Horn, published some considerable time before Vivier boasted his so-called discovery. Its explanation in this: When producing a tone with the tongue or the lips, one may at the same time emit another tone by singing, whether it be a higher or a lower one than the one played. Thus, while giving out the note *C* with the tongue, on the horn, the *E* above it, being a third higher, may be sung, and so on, as for instance:	En 1843, Vivier (Eugène) célèbre virtuose corniste et compositeur, fixa tout à coup l'attention publique sur lui, par la découverte qu'il fit d'un phénomène acoustique dont il n'a pas encore été donné une explication suffisante: ce phénomène consiste dans la production de plusieurs sons simultanés par le tube d'un cor, lesquels font harmonie consonnante, etc., etc. (Fétis, Biographie universelle des musiciens, tome 8, page 370.) Rien n'est plus facile à expliquer. D'abord la découverte ne doit pas en être attribué à Vivier, ce phénomène etait déjà connu de Ch. M. de Weber, qui l'a employé dans son Concertino pour Cor et orchestre, de plus le fameux corniste Dauprat en explique le mécanisme dans sa grande Méthode, publiée bien avant l'époque où Vivier fit parade de sa prétendue découverte. Voici, du reste, en quoi consiste le phénomène tant prôné: En même temps que l'on peut émettre un son avec la langue et les lèvres, on peut aussi chanter de la gorge, soit au dessus soit au dessous de la note que l'on donne sur le cor. Ainsi, si l'on frappe la note *ut*, on peut y joindre au moyen de la voix le *mi* au dessus, et ainsi de suite:

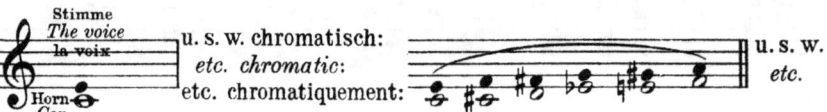

| Auf diese Art kann man auch die tiefere Note singen und dazu die höher liegende auf dem Instrumente spielen. | In like manner, the lower note may be sung and the higher one given out by the instrument. | De même on peut chanter la partie inférieure, et jouer avec le cor la partie supérieure. |

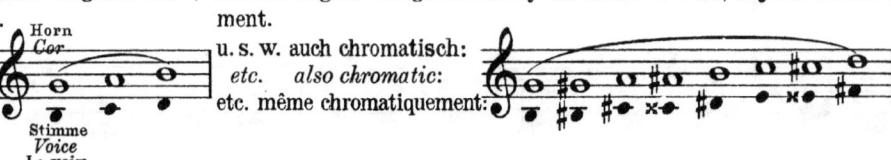

| Wenn man den Grundton auf dem Horn angibt z. B.: | If the fundamental note is given out on the horn, for instance: | Si l'on donne la note inférieure avec le Cor, par exemple: |

 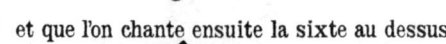

| und singt die Sexte: | and the sixth above it is sung: | et que l'on chante ensuite la sixte au dessus: |

  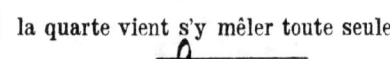

| so erklingt die Quarte von selbst: | the fourth will sound of its own accord: | la quarte vient s'y mêler toute seule: |

 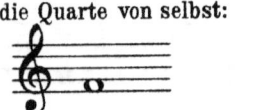

| und man erhält den vollständigen Akkord: | the result being a complete chord: | de cette façon on obtient un accord complet: |

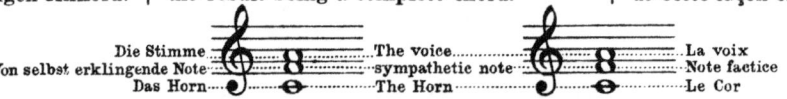

Ebenso wenn man *h* singt:	Again, if the *B* is sung:	De même si l'on chante le *si*:
und spielt *g* dazu:	and the *G* given out by the horn:	et que l'on donne le *sol* sur le Cor:
dann erklingt das *d* von selbst:	the *D* will sound likewise:	le *ré* vient tout naturellement:
und man hat den Akkord:	forming the perfect chord:	et forme un accord parfait:

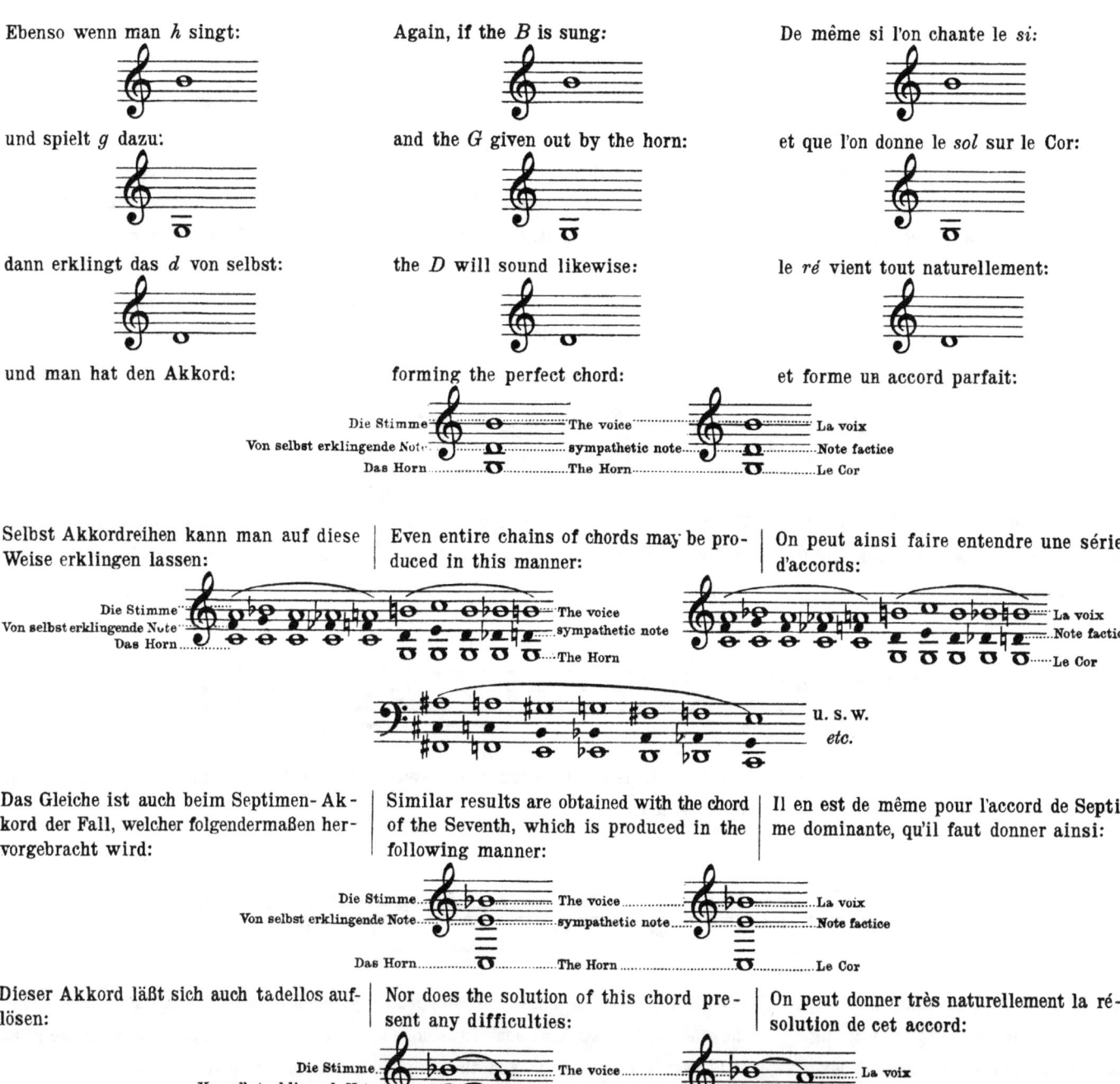

Selbst Akkordreihen kann man auf diese Weise erklingen lassen:	Even entire chains of chords may be produced in this manner:	On peut ainsi faire entendre une série d'accords:
Das Gleiche ist auch beim Septimen-Akkord der Fall, welcher folgendermaßen hervorgebracht wird:	Similar results are obtained with the chord of the Seventh, which is produced in the following manner:	Il en est de même pour l'accord de Septime dominante, qu'il faut donner ainsi:
Dieser Akkord läßt sich auch tadellos auflösen:	Nor does the solution of this chord present any difficulties:	On peut donner très naturellement la résolution de cet accord:
Nach dieser Anweisung kann man Duette oder Trios auf einem einzelnen Horne spielen, wenn man sonst guten Ansatz, eine, ein wenig gewandte Stimme mit gutem Gehör vereinigt, besitzt. Es wird dann möglich sein, recht gute und sogar recht hübsche Effekte, zu erzielen, welche das Publikum entzücken, es aber vorzüglich durch seine Unkenntnis dieses akustischen Phänomens in Erstaunen setzen. Indes werden wirkliche Künstler derartige Produktionen im Konzertsaale stets verachten. Das Ganze ist mehr Schwindel und wird nie den Beifall wahrhaft gebildeter Leute oder den wahrer Kenner erhalten.	In this way, a duet or a trio may be performed, on one horn only, by a fairly expert player, possessing a somewhat flexible voice combined with an accurate ear. He will thus be enabled to produce some very happy and even surprising effects, calculated to delight and astonish an audience unfamiliar with this acoustic phenomenon. On the other hand, serious artists will ever abstain from similar exhibitions in the concert-room. They are, after all, a species of trickery and charlatanism, which will not meet with the approval of cultured amateurs and true connoisseurs.	De cette manière on peut exécuter soit un Duo, soit un Trio sur un Cor seul, pour peu que l'on soit en possession d'une bonne embouchure, c'est-à-dire de bonnes lèvres, et d'une voix un peu agile jointe à une oreille juste, il est possible alors de produire de très heureux et même de jolis effets, qui peuvent charmer et surtout étonner le public, peu initié au sujet de ce phénomène acoustique. Toutefois les artistes sérieux devront dédaigner ces sortes de productions dans une salle de concert, car le procédé sent toujours un peu trop le charlatanisme, et ne pourra jamais obtenir l'approbation des gens de goût, ni des vrais connaisseurs.

Das Echo	The Production of the Echo	De l'Echo, que l'on peut produire sur le cor
Man erzeugt das Echo auf dem Naturhorn durch einen, in den Becher gesteckten Dämpfer von leichtem Holze oder von Pappe. Noch leichter macht sich die Sache auf dem chromatischen Horne. Man schlage folgendes Verfahren ein:	The echo effect is produced by the insertion, in the bell of the Natural Horn, of a sourdine or muffler, made of light wood or cardboard. In the case of the chromatic Horn, the procedure is yet more simple, as under:	On peut produire l'Echo, en adoptant dans le pavillon du Cor simple, une sourdine faite en bois léger ou en carton. Pour le Cor à pistons ou à cylindres, la chose présente plus de facilité. On procède de la manière suivante:

| Die vorstehende Stelle als Echo mit heruntergedrücktem, zweiten Ventile und gestopftem Trichter: | The same passage, as an echo, with the second ventil pressed down and the bell hand-stopped: | Le même passage en Echo, baissez le IIme piston, et bouchez le pavillon avec la main: |

| In Wirklichkeit spielt man demnach auf E-Horn: | In reality, therefore, the passage is played, on the E horn: | On joue donc en réalité sur le cor en mi♮: |

| da alle Noten gestopft sind; der Eindruck ist packend und von großer Wirkung. Es versteht sich von selbst, daß das, was hier über die mehrfachen Töne, sowie über das Echo gesagt ist, mit geringen Ausnahmen auf allen Bogen auszuführen ist. Die schönsten und sich am besten dazu eignenden Bogen jedoch sind *Es*, *E* und *F*, welche am brillantesten klingen, und auch leicht zu spielen sind. Der *G-Bogen*, obwohl sehr schön, ist dennoch ein wenig zu schmetternd für Solo. *D*, *Des* und *C* sind zu dumpf, und *As*, *A*, *B* und *H* sind zu grell und auch schwer zu spielen. | inasmuch as all the notes are "stopped"; the effect is both striking and picturesque. It is hardly necessary to add, that what has here been said with regard to double and triple tones, as well as to the echo effect, applies equally, with but few exceptions, to all the crooks. Of the latter, however, the most suitable and effective are the *E flat*, the *E* and the *F* crooks, as being the most brilliant and at the same time the easiest to manage. The *G* crook, although very brilliant, is rather too blatant for solo playing. The *D*, *D flat*, and *C* crooks, on the other hand, are too dull, and those for *A flat*, *A*, *B flat* and *B* too shrill, and moreover difficult to play. | puisque toutes les notes se trouvent bouchées avec la main; l'effet est de plus saisissant et pittoresque. Il va sans dire que tout ce que je viens d'indiquer sur les doubles et triples sons, ainsi que sur l'Echo, peut se reproduire à peu près sur tous les tons de rechange. Parmi les plus beaux tons on remarque les tons de *Mi♭*, *Mi♮* et *Fa*, qui sont les plus brillants et les plus agréables à jouer. Le ton de *Sol*, quoique très joli, est cependant un peu éclatant pour le Solo. Les tons de *Ré♮*, *Ré♭* et *Ut*, sont trop sourds, et ceux de *La♭*, *La♮*, *Si♭* et *Si♮* haut, trop aigus, criards et difficiles à jouer. |

Praktische Ratschläge für den Orchestermusiker	Practical Hints to the Orchestral Artist	Conseils pratiques pour l'artiste de l'orchestre
Die Stellung des Waldhornisten im modernen Orchester ist eine ziemlich schwierige und erfordert viele Vorsicht, um die angewiesene Partie recht künstlerisch zur Geltung zu bringen.	The position of the hornist in the modern orchestra is not by any means an easy one to hold and requires much care and circumspection if he would perform the part allotted to him in a truly artistic manner.	La place de cor dans l'orchestre moderne est assez difficile à tenir et demande beaucoup de prudence pour pouvoir exécuter les parties d'une façon convenable.
Vor allem muß das Bestreben des ausübenden Hornisten darauf ausgehen, jedesmal beim Eintritt einer wichtigen Stelle sich stets eines guten Anstoßes des zu gebenden Tones im Voraus zu versichern. So z. B. beim Eintritt des Solohornquartetts in der Freischütz-Ouvertüre:	It should be his endeavour, in the first place, to ensure, at every important entry of his part, a ready attack, and a firm, steady tone. Thus, for instance, in the entry of the quartet for horn soli, in the overture of "Der Freischütz".	Il est de toute nécessité pour le corniste de s'assurer à chaque entrée de l'attaque ferme du son, pour éviter de faire un couac. Ainsi, par exemple, dans l'entrée du quatuor solo, dans l'ouverture du Freyschütz:

Der Einsatz der 2 ersten Hörner im 5. Takt ist sehr schwierig, weil besonders das hohe G des 1. Hornes und auch mitunter das E des 2. Hornes leicht überschlagen; um dieser unangenehmen Wirkung vorzubeugen, rate ich den 2 ersten Hornisten, ganz leise einige Noten mit dem 3. u. 4. Horn mitzublasen, so vorbereitet wird der hohe Einsatz gewiß nicht überschlagen.	The entry of the two horns in the fifth bar, is a most difficult test, the high G, of the first horn, and sometimes also the E, of the second, being very liable to give over. In order to avoid this unpleasant contretemps, I should advise the two first hornists to play, quite softly, a few preliminary notes with the third and fourth horns. Thus prepared, the attack of the high notes will be rendered the more certain.	L'attaque des sons élevés *sol* et *mi* est pour les 2 premiers cors très difficile et sujet à couacer; pour éviter cet effet désagréable, je conseille aux 2 premiers cors, de jouer pianissimo quelques notes avec les 3e. et 4e. cors. Ainsi préparé, l'attaque des sons élevés se fera sans rater.
Bei Stellen, wo solche Vorbereitung nicht möglich ist, muß das Mundstück frühzeitig genug angesetzt werden, um gleich in den richtigen Ton einzufallen; so im folgenden Satz der Pastoralsymphonie von Beethoven, welcher gar nicht leicht zu blasen ist:	In passages where a similar preparation is not feasible, the mouthpiece should be placed in position on the lips in ample time to enable the player to attack the desired note with certainty. This applies, for example, to the following, by no means easy, passage in Beethoven's "Pastoral-Symphony":	Dans des passages, où une semblable préparation n'est pas praticable, on devra mettre l'embouchure assez tôt aux lèvres pour pouvoir attaquer d'une manière certaine le ton voulu. Ainsi dans le passage suivant, de la Symphonie Pastorale, de Beethoven, lequel n'est pas facile à jouer, il faut bien préparer l'embouchure pour être en mesure d'attaquer sans hésitation:

Ein höchst schwieriger Eintritt ist der folgende im Adagio der B-dur Symphonie von Beethoven, welcher nach 9 Takten Pausen *pp* geblasen werden soll.	A most difficult entry for the horns occurs in the B flat major symphony of the same composer, where, after nine bars of rest, the C is to be given out pianissimo:	Une bien difficile rentrée est la suivante, qui se trouve dans l'Adagio de la Symphonie en Si♭ majeur de Beethoven, où, après 9 mesures de silences, on doit attaquer *pp* l'ut supérieur:

Die Haltung der rechten Hand im Becher soll nach der in dieser Schule mitgeteilten Vorschrift stets genau beobachtet werden, was der Mehrzahl der heutigen Hornisten ganz unbekannt ist, deswegen die Zahl der echten Hornbläser immer geringer wird.

So las ich neulich in einer Hornschule folgendes: „Bei dem Ventilhorn hat die rechte Hand eine andere Funktion, indem die 3 mittleren Finger derselben die Ventile zu regieren haben und sie nur dann sich in den Schallbecher verfügt, wenn ein Ton gestopft werden soll."

Ein solches Verfahren muß zu einem wirklich ganz kuriosen Hornblasen führen. Der Verfasser dieser „Hornschule"(!!!) hat nie in seinem Leben ein Horn in den Händen gehalten, geschweige denn geblasen.

Das präzise Anschlagen des zu gebenden Tones, sowie die schöne Haltung der rechten Hand im Becher, verleiht dem Horn seinen Hauptreiz, welcher in einem schönen, wohlklingeden, zu Herzen der Zuhörer dringenden Ton besteht.

Um sich stets einen guten Ansatz zu sichern, ist es ratsam, folgende Vorschriften zu befolgen:

Das Mundstück ist, wenn man zu blasen aufhört, sowie ehe man anfängt, sorgsam durch Abreiben, z. B. mit einem wollenen Tuche, zu reinigen, damit sich nichts Schädliches ansetzen kann.

Man hüte sich auf dem Mundstück eines Andern zu blasen, wenn es noch feucht, nicht gehörig gereinigt, oder noch warm ist; in diesen Fällen bekommt man leicht einen bösen Mund; darum ist auch das Wegleihen des Mundstückes immer sehr bedenklich.

Man halte sein Instrument immer rein vom Staube, der sich leicht mit dem in dasselbe laufenden Wasser vermischt, und so durch Schmutz der Reinheit des Tones, sowie seiner Güte nachteilig ist. Nach dem Blasen lasse man daher das Wasser aus dem Instrument ganz ablaufen, aber nicht so, daß es durch die Röhre dringt, sonst setzt sich leicht der der Gesundheit des Bläsers sowie dem Instrument selbst gleich nachteilige Grünspan an. Oft sammelt sich während des Blasens zu viel Wasser in dem Instrumente, was man durch das Röcheln desselben leicht bemerkt und welches die Reinheit des Tones sehr nachteilig beeinflußt und die Töne leicht überschlagen läßt; bei einer kleineren oder größeren Pause lasse man es daher ablaufen, aber nicht durch das Mundstück, was wirklich ganz abscheulich ist, und an welchem Verfahren man gleich den gemeinen Musikanten erkennt.

The position of the right hand in the bell of the instrument should be regulated strictly in accordance with the instructions contained in this "School", albeit by the great majority of hornists in the present day this important particular is entirely ignored— one of the reasons, indeed, for the increasing scarcity of competent horn-players.

Some time since, I happened upon the following passage in a "Method for the Horn":_ "In the case of the Ventil Horn, the right hand performs another function; the three middle fingers being employed in manipulating the valves, while the hand is only placed in the bell of the instrument when a tone requires to be stopped".

Such a procedure must indeed be productive of some rather singular "virtuosity" in horn-playing. It may be asserted, with some confidence, that the author of this "Method"(!) has in all probability never held a horn in his hand, or been within measurable distance of playing it.

The accuracy of tone-production, as well as the proper holding of the hand in the bell of the instrument, impart to the horn its distinctive charm, which consists in a truly melodious and sympathetic tone.

In order always to ensure the efficiency of the instrument, the following precautions should be habitually observed:_

The mouthpiece, both before and after being used, should be carefully cleaned with, say, a piece of flannel.

Avoid using the mouthpiece of another person, particularly if still moist or not sufficiently clean; soreness of the lips and other complaints may otherwise be contracted. For a similar reason one's own mouthpiece should not be lent to another person, particularly a stranger.

The instrument should be kept free from dust, which mixing with the moisture accumulating in the tubes, soon affects the purity of the tone. After playing, the accumulated moisture should be carefully discharged, as if allowed to remain for any length of time, verdigris is apt to form in the tubes and joints, which will not only unfavourably affect the condition of the instrument, but may likewise prove injurious to the health of the player. Sometimes, an excessive quantity of moisture will collect in the instrument during a performance, (easily detected by a gurgling sound in the tube) interfering with the purity of the tone and the steadiness of its production. In that case, during the first convenient pause, the moisture should be discharged; but not before having first removed the mouthpiece, as the practice of allowing it to pass through the latter is a most reprehensible one and indicative of a low breeding.

La tenue de la main droite dans le Pavillon de l'instrument, doit être, d'après la règle donnée dans cette méthode, toujours rigoureusement observée, quoique cette particularité importante soit inconnue à la plupart des cornistes de notre époque, ce qui est une des causes du nombre toujours plus restreint de bons cornistes.

Je lisais dernièrement dans une méthode de cor, le passage suivant: „Avec le cor à pistons, la main droite a une autre fonction; les 3 doigts du milieu servent à faire mouvoir le mécanisme des 3 pistons et ne se place dans le pavillon de l'instrument si l'un des sons doit être bouché.

Une semblable manière de tenir le cor doit produire un effet curieux. L'auteur de cette méthode (!!!) n'a probablement jamais tenu un cor dans ses mains ni essayé d'en jouer!

L'attaque précise du son, ainsi qu'une jolie tenue de la main droite dans le pavillon de l'instrument, donne au cor ce charme particulier qui consiste en une belle qualité de son.

Pour s'assurer de lèvres solides, il est urgent de suivre ces quelques conseils:

Lorsqu'on a terminé de jouer, on essuiera soigneusement l'embouchure.

Il ne faut jamais se servir de l'embouchure d'une autre personne, autrement on s'expose à attraper mal aux lèvres ou d'autres maux pires encore. Ne prêtez jamais votre embouchure à une personne étrangère.

Il faut toujours tenir son instrument dans un état de propreté convenable.

Après avoir joué, il faut laisser écouler l'eau hors de l'instrument; sans cette précaution, il se formera par suite de l'accumulation de l'eau dans les conduits, le vert-de-gris, qui altère non seulement la qualité de l'instrument mais est aussi funeste à la santé de l'exécutant. Pendant que l'on joue, l'eau s'amasse dans l'instrument; à ce moment le son s'altère et devient vacillant, ce qui favorise les couacs; on profitera d'un silence indiqué pour faire écouler l'eau hors de l'instrument. Cette opération doit se faire en ôtant l'embouchure, car faire écouler l'eau par l'embouchure est tout simplement malpropre et digne seulement d'un musicien de foire.

Die Züge und Kulissen des Instruments sind durch Einschmieren mit einer fettartigen Materie, die aber nicht gerinnen darf, stets in einem solchen Zustande zu erhalten, daß sie sehr leicht zu bewegen sind; das beste hierzu ist Oliven-Oel, dabei hüte man sich aber, die Pistons oder Ventile mit Oel einzureiben; das einfachste Mittel, damit sie immer einen gleichartigen sanften Gang beim Niederdrükken und Aufschnellen beibehalten, ist einfach, diese mit Wasser oder auch Speichel zu benetzen. Ist der Mund des Bläsers rissig geworden, so kann man sich der Mundpomade bedienen, außerdem ist Essig mit Wasser vermischt sehr gut, er zieht zusammen und gibt einen guten Ansatz. Das Rauchen sowie Biertrinken in Zwischenakten bei Opern und Konzertaufführungen soll unterlassen werden, denn das ist den Lippen sehr schädlich.

Die in neuerer Zeit gemachte Behauptung, daß die Anwendung von Bogen beim Ventilhorn absolut widersinnig sei und daß man alles auf dem *F-Horn* zu transponieren habe, ist falsch und rührt von solchen Leuten her, die von der wahren Beschaffenheit des Waldhornes keinen richtigen Begriff haben.

Durch ein solches schablones Verfahren geraten die meisten Hornisten, welche in der *F*-Stimmung verharren und transponieren, in eine ganz unangenehme Lage, so daß sie gewöhnlich solche Sätze verpatzen und sich dem allgemeinen Gelächter der Zuhörer preisgeben.

Ich rate die *G*, *A* und hoch *B*-Stimmung so oft als möglich aufzustecken, dadurch erleichtert man sich manche schwierige Stelle, die auf dem vorgeschriebenen Bogen besser auszuführen ist und auch dabei reiner klingt, als wenn man sie auf dem *F-Bogen* transponiert. Nachstehende Beispiele soll man, anstatt auf dem *F-Bogen* zu transponieren, in der vorgeschriebenen Stimmung blasen:

D-dur Symphonie. Auf dem *A-Bogen* leicht ausführbar:

The sliding gear of the instrument should be maintained in good working condition by the frequent application of some non-coagulative lubricant; olive oil being the most effective for the purpose. The pistons or ventils, on the other hand, must be kept altogether free from oil, the simplest means of preserving the "springiness" of the latter being to moisten them from time to time with water or with saliva.

For the cure of cracked or slightly inflamed lips, the use of a little coldcream is to be recommended; a mixture of vinegar and water is likewise very serviceable, as it contracts the lips and thus imparts firmness to them. The consumption of beer, or a habit of smoking, during the entr'acts and intervals in operatic or concert performances, should not be indulged in, as it is most injurious to the lips of the horn-player.

The assertion, which has been absurdly made in recent times, that the use of the crooks in connection with the Ventil horn should be discontinued, as being absolutely useless, since everything could be transposed on the *F*-horn, is not worth serious consideration.

Hornists who follow such mischievous advice by attempting to transpose all passages on the *F* horn, will find themselves frequently coming to grief and exposing themselves to the ridicule of their audience.

I advise the employment of the *G*, the *A*, and the high *B* flat crooks whenever these are indicated by the composer. By their aid, the passages will be rendered with greater ease, more clearly and with a truer tone than when they are transposed on the *F* horn.

The subjoined examples, to be executed with the crooks indicated, may serve by way of illustration:

Symphony in *D major*, easily playable with the *A* crook:

Les coulisses de l'instrument doivent êtres toujours en bon état, il faut qu'on puisse les tirer avec facilité; à cette fin, on les enduit d'une légère couche d'une matière graisseuse, comme du sindoux ou l'huile d'olive fine.

On évitera soigneusement que la graisse ou l'huile ne s'introduisent pas dans les pistons; pour rendre ces derniers élastiques, il suffit de les humecter, de temps à autre, simplement avec un peu d'eau ou de salive.

Si les lèvres s'enflamment et deviennent malades, il suffit pour les guérir d'appliquer un peu de pommade rose ou du Goldcream. Une lotion de vinaigre mélangé avec de l'eau, est aussi très propice à rendre aux lèvres leurs forces et donner une bonne embouchure.

Pendant les Entr'actes d'un opéra ou d'un concert, il faut s'abstenir de fumer et de boire de la bière, cela ne convient pas bien aux lèvres.

L'opinion de quelques uns qui considèrent l'emploi des tons de rechange comme inutile, puisque on peut tout transposer sur le cor chromatique avec le ton de *Fa* ne doit pas être prise en considération, car elle est absurde. Ceux qui la préconisent méconnaissent le caractère réel du cor.

Les cornistes qui suivent de semblables conseils, en transposant tous les passages sur le ton de *Fa*, s'exposent souvent à devenir la risée des auditeurs.

Je conseille d'employer les tons de rechange de *Sol*, *La* et de *Si♭* haut, s'ils sont prescrits par le compositeur. De cette façon, les passages se feront facilement et seront aussi plus justes que transposés sur le ton de *Fa*.

Les exemples suivants doivent se faire sur les tons de rechange prescrits:

Symphonie en *re-maj*. Sur le ton de *La* facile à exécuter:

Auf dem *F-Horn* transponiert, bietet große Schwierigkeit, besonders für das 1. Horn:

Transposed on the *F* horn, it presents great difficulties, particularly to the first horn:

Transposé sur le ton de *Fa*, offre de grandes difficultés, surtout pour le 1. cor:

78

| *G-moll* Symphonie. Auf dem *G-Bogen* leicht ausführbar: | *G minor* Symphony. Easily playable with the *G* crook: | Symphonie en *sol-min*. Sur le ton de *sol* facile à exécuter: |

Auf dem *F-Horn* transponiert, bietet große Schwierigkeit, besonders für das 1. Horn: | Presents great difficulties if transposed on the *F* horn, particularly to the first horn: | Transposé sur le ton de *Fa*, offre de grandes difficultés, surtout pour le 1. cor:

Jagdouvertüre. Auf dem *A-Bogen* leicht ausführbar: | Ouverture de Chasse. Easily playable with the *A* crook: | Ouverture de Chasse. Sur le ton de *La* facile à exécuter:

Auf dem *F-Horn* schwierig auszuführen: | Difficult of execution on the *F* horn: | Sur le ton de *Fa* très difficile à jouer:

A-moll Symphonie, auf *A-Bogen* leicht ausführbar: | *A minor* Symphony. Easily playable with the *A* crook: | Symphonie en *La-min*. Sur le ton de *La* facile à exécuter:

Auf dem *F-Horn* schwierig auszuführen: | Difficult of execution on the *F* horn: | Sur le ton de *Fa* difficile à exécuter:

| Auf dem *G-Bogen* leicht ausführbar: | Easily playable with the *G* crook: | Sur le ton de *sol* facile à exécuter: |

| Schwer zu blasen auf *F-Bogen* transponiert: | Difficult if transposed on the *F* horn: | Sur le ton de *Fa* d'une exécution difficile: |

| Auf dem *G-Bogen* leicht ausführbar: | Easily playable with the *G* crook: | Sur le ton de *sol*, exécution facile et brillante: |

| Auf dem *F-Bogen* sehr schwer zu blasen: | Difficult if transposed on the *F* horn: | Sur le ton de *Fa* d'une grande difficulté à exécuter: |

| Folgender Satz läßt sich wegen des Trillers besser auf dem *Es-Bogen* blasen. | The following passage, because of the shake, is preferably produced on the *E flat* crook. | A cause du Trille, il est préférable de jouer le *solo* suivant sur le ton prescrit. |

| Ebenso klingt folgender Satz bedeutend brillanter und ist leichter zu blasen auf dem *G-Bogen*, als auf *F-Bogen* transponiert ausgeführt. | The following example also is more readily produced on the *G* crook, than transposed on the *F* horn. | Le passage suivant est plus facile à exécuter sur le ton de *Sol*, au lieu de le transposer sur le ton de *Fa*. |

Es gibt viele Hornisten, die, wenn der Dienst zu Ende ist, ihr Instrument bis zum nächsten Dienste nicht mehr anrühren. Derartige Leute behandeln eben die Kunst wie ein Handwerk; der wahre Künstler aber wird in der Zwischenzeit, wo er keinen Dienst zu leisten hat, auf seinem Instrumente entweder eine Etüde oder einige Präludien oder Sonaten blasen, um sich eines guten Ansatzes zu versichern, denn nur in solcher Weise werden ihm abends bei der Aufführung die etwaigen vorkommenden Solopassagen ohne Mühe gelingen. Was mich betrifft, so habe ich diesen Rat immer befolgt und mich wohl dabei befunden.

There are many hornists who, when their professional duties for the time being are discharged, will not touch the instrument until again called upon to do so by their engagements. Such individuals reduce their art to the level of a mere handicraft. The true artist, on the other hand, will be careful to keep himself in constant training by playing, during the intervals of his engagements, an etude, a few preludes or sonatas etc; for only in this way will he be enabled to render full justice to any solo passages allotted to him in performance, and to attack his part in the orchestra with confidence. This is a rule which I have always observed myself, and I have found it answer well.

Il y a beaucoup de cornistes qui, une fois le service terminé, ne touchent plus à leur instrument. Ces sortes de gens considèrent l'art comme un métier; le vrai artiste, au contraire, saura mettre à profit l'intervalle qui s'écoule d'un service à l'autre, pour jouer une Etude ou quelques Préludes et Gammes, pour se maintenir une bonne embouchure qui lui permettra le soir à l'exécution, de faire sans peine ni ratures les passages les plus difficiles. En ce qui me concerne, j'ai toujours suivi cette manière de faire et je m'en suis bien trouvé.

Waren für die Aufführung einige schwierige Stellen in Aussicht, so probierte ich diese jedesmal vorerst zu Hause; auf diese Art versagte mir nie weder der Ansatz noch die tadellose Wiedergabe der betreffenden Solostellen und wurde gewöhnlich meine Bemühung vom Publikum mit ungeteiltem Beifallsklatschen belohnt.

Zum Schluß will ich noch eine Aufklärung über die, in alten italienischen Orchesterstimmen sich vorfindende Bezeichnung der verschiedenen Bogen geben.

Die Bogen für Kreuztonarten wurden mit *C sol fa ut, G sol ré ut, D la sol ré, A la mi ré*, u. s. w. bezeichnet. Durch diese Benennung wurde die Tonika, die Dominante und die Unterdominante der Tonart gekennzeichnet.

Die Bogen für *B* Tonarten wurden mit *E la fa, A la fa, D la fa, G la fa* bezeichnet, was sich auf folgenden Beweggrund stützte: Das letzte *B* dieser Tonarten, welches sich auf der 4. Stufe befindet, heißt immer *F*, weil dieses *F* die höher liegende Note des ersten Halbtons ist; indem nun die Tonika durch den ersten Buchstaben angegeben, ist es sehr leicht herauszufinden, welche Note durch ein *B* erniedrigt wird; diese Note wird immer mit *F* bezeichnet, dadurch wird die Aufmerksamkeit auf diese Note geleitet, indem sie immer *F* genannt wird.

So ist *F* der *Es-dur* Tonart *As; F* der *As-dur* Tonart *Des; F* der *Des-dur* Tonart *Ges,* und *F* der *Ges-dur* Tonart *Ces.*

Was nun die Bezeichnung *La*, welche vor *Fa* steht, anlangt und welche zur Angabe der Tonarten *E la fa, A la fa, D la fa,* u. s. w. dient, so ist anzunehmen, daß *La* entweder die Tonika, oder die 4. Stufe, oder auch die Dominante dadurch andeuten will. So ist für *E la fa, La* die Unterdominante; für *A la fa* ist *La* die Tonika; für *D la fa* ist *La* als Dominante zu verstehen.

Bei *G la fa* aber ist diese Bezeichnung unerklärlich; wahrscheinlich hat sich diese Bezeichnung durch Schlendrian eingeschlichen oder stammt von einer falschen Auffaßung her.

Wie dem auch sei, diese veralteten lächerlichen Benennungen sind in den neueren italienischen Partituren für immer verschwunden.

Whenever at some prospective performance some difficult solo passages happened to be included in the horn part, I invariably played them over at home first, and was rewarded eventually, for a faultless rendering, by the encouraging applause of the audience.

A brief explanation of the indications for the change of Keys, to be found in old Italian orchestral horn parts, may here be given, by way of conclusion:

The crooks for the sharp Keys are indicated by *C sol fa ut, G sol re ut, D la sol re, A la mi re*, etc.; under which denominations the Tonic, the Dominant, and the Sub-Dominant were to be understood.

The crooks for the flat Keys are indicated by *E la fa, A la fa, G la fa*, which is to be explained as follows: The last *flat* of these Keys, being on the fourth degree, is always called *F*, since this *F* is the note above the first semitone. Thus, the Tonic being indicated by the first letter, it is easy to find out which note is lowered by the *flat* and thus becomes *F*, and it is for this reason attention is drawn to this note by calling it *F* throughout. Thus, *F*, of the Key of *E flat major* is *A flat; F* of the Key of *A flat major* is *D flat; F* of *D flat major* is *G flat;* and *F* of *G flat major* is *C flat.*

As regards the designation of *La*, which precedes the *Fa*, and which serves to indicate the Keys *E la fa, A la fa, D la fa* etc., it must be assumed that *la* either refers to the Tonic, or the fourth degree, or the Dominant. Thus in the case of *E la fa, la* represents the Sub-Dominant; in that of *A la fa, la* is the Tonic; and in *D la fa, la* means the Dominant.

In the case of *G la fa*, the designation is inexplicable and probably the result of some confused usage or false analogy. In any case, these obsolete and sufficiently absurd denominations have fortunately fallen in disuse and are no longer to be met with in the scores of modern Italian masters.

Si quelques passages ou Soli étaient en perspective, je prenais soin de les étudier au préalable, à la maison, de cette façon je ne manquais jamais ni d'embouchure ni de sûreté dans l'exécution de ces soli et le public récompensait généralement ma peine par des applaudissements encourageants.

Pour finir, je veux donner une explication sur les dénominations des tons de rechange qui se trouvent indiquées dans certaines vieilles parties d'orchestre italiennes.

Les tons de rechange par dièses s'appellent *C sol fa ut, G sol ré ut, D la sol ré, A la mi ré*, etc. c'était pour faire connaître les noms de la tonique, de la dominante et de la sous-dominante; la dénomination des tons de rechange par bémols, *E la fa, A la fa, D la fa, G la fa* sont fondées sur les raisons suivantes: Le dernier bémol de ces tons étant sur le 4. degré est toujours *fa*, puisque c'est la note supérieure au demi-ton; or, connaissant la tonique par la lettre, on trouve à l'instant quelle est la note bémolisée qui devient *fa*, et c'est pour cela qu'on appelle l'attention sur cette note en disant *Fa* pour chaque ton.

Ainsi *Fa* du ton de *mi*♭, est *la*♭; *fa* du ton de *la*♭, est *ré*♭; *fa* du ton de *ré*♭, est *sol*♭; enfin *fa* du ton de *sol*♭, est *ut*♭.

A l'égard du nom de *la* qui précède celui de *fa* dans la désignation des tons *E la fa, A la fa, D la fa*, je pense, que c'est pour indiquer dans tous ces tons que *la* est toujours ou la tonique, ou le 4ᵉ degré, ou la dominante. Ainsi, dans *E la fa*, la est la sous-dominante; dans *A la fa*, c'est la tonique; dans *D la fa* c'est la dominante.

J'avoue cependant que dans *G la fa*, il me paraît inexplicable. Je présume qu'il s'y est glissé que par un usage peu réfléchi ou par une apparence d'analogie mal raisonnée.

Comme qu'il en soit, ces vieilles dénominations sont complètement tombées en désuétude et ne se trouvent plus jamais employées dans les partitions modernes des maîtres italiens.

Sechs charakteristische Studien und sechs große Präludien

Trotzdem die folgenden Studien eigentlich für Naturhorn geschrieben sind, so empfehle ich sie doch auch denen, welche sich des Ventilhorns bedienen. Die zu überwindenden Schwierigkeiten sind auf beiden Instrumenten dieselben. Die nachfolgenden Präludien sind besonders für Ventilhorn geschrieben.

Betonung, Nüancierung, Rhythmus, mit einem Wort ausdrucksvoller Vortrag, das ist, was man vor allen Dingen beim Studium von Stücken wie den folgenden beobachten muß. Die schönsten Musikstücke, ausdruckslos vorgetragen, sind nichts als tote Buchstaben.

Das Horn ist im höchsten Sinne des Wortes ein schönes Instrument. Es eignet sich eben so gut zu Hirten- wie Waldszenen; das Geheimnisvolle, Märchenhafte ist ihm so wenig fremd wie das Leidenschaftliche. Frisch denn an's Werk, Ihr Jünglinge, Ihr, die Ihr wahre Künstler werden wollt, sucht Eure Zuhörer zu rühren! Gelingt Euch dies, so seid Ihr des Erfolges sicher.

Six Characteristic Studies and Six grand Preludes

Although the subjoined studies have been originally written for the Natural Horn, they may be nevertheless recommended also to the player of the Ventil Horn. The difficulties to be surmounted are the same in both cases. The six preludes which follow, are intended specially for the Ventil Horn.

Particular attention should be paid in the study of pieces of this description to **accent, rhythm,** and **phrasing,** or, in other words, to a truly **expressive** rendering. The finest musical composition, rendered without true feeling and expression, is but a meaningless series of so many notes.

The horn may be justly called a beautiful instrument in the highest sense of the word. It lends itself equally well to the illustration of pastoral and forest scenes; to suggestions of the romantic and the mysterious, and to the accents of passion and of pathos. It is worthy, then, of your diligent and persevering efforts, young pupils, this instrument of your choice!

And if you aspire one day to become true artists, endeavour to move the hearts of your audience; if you are able to do that, your success is assured.

Six études caractéristiques et Six grands Préludes

Quoique les études suivantes aient été spécialement écrites en vue du cor simple, je les conseille aussi à ceux des élèves qui se servent du cor chromatique, car les difficultés à vaincre sont les mêmes pour les deux instruments.

Les six Préludes qui suivent s'adressent plus particulièrement au cor chromatique. Ce qu'il faut avant tout observer dans l'étude des morceaux du genre de ceux qui suivent, c'est de bien les **accentuer,** nuancer et **rhythmer,** en un mot de les exécuter d'une manière **expressive,** car sans l'expression la musique la plus belle n'est plus qu'une lettre morte.

Le cor est l'instrument par excellence qui se prête également aux scènes pastorales, forestières, féeriques, dramatiques et pathétiques.

Courage donc, jeunes élèves, vous qui aspirez à devenir un jour des artistes sérieux, tâchez d'émouvoir votre auditoire et alors le succès ne vous fera pas défaut.

Sechs charakteristische Studien / Six Characteristic Studies / Six études caractéristiques

Allegro agitato.

2.

Tema con variazioni.
Andante con moto.

6.

p

cresc.

Var. I.

Var. II.

Sechs große Präludien | Six grand Preludes | Six grands Préludes

92

5. Moderato.

www.ingramcontent.com/pod-product-compliance
Lightning Source LLC
Chambersburg PA
CBHW082014220426
43670CB00015B/2627